Solange Berchemin | Martin Dunford

111 Places
in Greenwich
That You
Shouldn't Miss

Photographs by Karin Tearle

T0150541

emons:

© Emons Verlag GmbH
All rights reserved
© Photographs by Karin Tearle, except:
Caird Library (ch. 7): courtesy of RMG
National Maritime Museum (ch. 50): courtesy of RMG
Old Brewery (ch. 53): Martin Dunford
Tulip Staircase, Queen's House (ch. 70): courtesy of RMG
Royal Blackheath Golf Club (ch. 79): courtesy of the Royal Blackheath Golf Club
St Paul's Church (ch. 92): Karin Tearle, with the permission
of the PCC of St Paul's, Deptford
Titanic Memorial (ch. 97): courtesy of RMG
Statue of Yuri Gargarin (ch. 111): courtesy of RMG
Layout: Editorial Design & Artdirection, Conny Laue, Bochum,
based on a design by Lübbeke | Naumann | Thoben
Maps: altancicek.design, www.altancicek.de
Basic cartographical information from Openstreetmap,
© OpenStreetMap-Mitwirkende, OdbL
Editing: Martin Sketchley
Printing and binding: Grafisches Centrum Cuno, Calbe
Printed in Germany 2021
ISBN 978-3-7408-1107-5
First edition

Did you enjoy this guidebook? Would you like to see more?
Join us in uncovering new places around the world on:
www.111places.com

Foreword

As the birthplace of Elizabeth I and even time itself, Greenwich – Royal Borough, home to the Prime Meridian, a UNESCO World Heritage Site – is one of London's most historic neighbourhoods, with some of the capital's most compelling sights. Unlike much of central London, however, Greenwich is a village at heart, and one that tourists flock to in growing numbers every year. We have of course written this book with them in mind. But, equally, we wrote it for those who call this amazing corner of London home, and who, like us, wouldn't live anywhere else. We also wrote it for ourselves. The more stories we found, the more we fell in love with Greenwich all over again – with its people, its history, and most of all its ravishing locations. We hope that you will too.

We've deliberately included world-famous places such as the *Cutty Sark* and the Painted Hall, going behind the scenes to reveal their lesser-known features and more offbeat tales: after all, what would Greenwich be without its links to the Thames and its naval heroes? But we've also included places that are so far off the tourist track as to be almost invisible: street corners that commemorate war heroes, suffragettes and rock-and-rollers; secret places to which we take our friends and families to avoid the crowds – a walk in Maryon Park, a paddle in Deptford Creek, and of course our favourite riverside pubs. And we make no apology for occasionally straying beyond the boundaries of the borough to visit places that remain an integral part of Greenwich's rich history – places that recall historical figures such as William Morris and Henry VIII, or Tom Cribb, the first-ever world champion bare-knuckle fighter. We even visit London's most famous sewage plant!

So take the 111 Places Challenge, explore the Royal Borough of Greenwich, and be prepared to fall in love.

111 Places

1 Albury Street, Deptford

Pretty street that's a keeper of secrets

Before Henry VIII used the site for his royal dock, Deptford was just a fishing village, but from then on it prospered, and in its heyday the High Street was the Oxford Street of South London. In early 1836, Deptford station was the first railway station to offer rail travel to Central London. The area was badly damaged during World War II, however, and went downhill from then. Demolition firms and unscrupulous developers teamed up to bulldoze entire streets to make way for high-rise tower blocks. In this context, finding an almost intact row of houses dating back to 1707 is nothing short of a miracle. Although Albury Street is geographically in the borough of Lewisham, it's so near the Greenwich boundary, and its own story so very intriguing, that it's one not to miss.

The first things you'll notice on entering the street are the cobbles and doorways, with their distinctive features: wooden canopies and sculpted brackets with cute cherubs. They were carved and restored by the best woodworkers in the land. If they seem to be arranged in a strange order, it's due to a mix-up 20 years ago, when the houses were auctioned. Albury Street's original residents were mostly senior naval officers. Evidence indicates that Lord Nelson would have stayed at number 19 – now 34 – when on leave. There's probably nothing exceptional to read into this – even a hero needs a crash pad – but Lady Hamilton is reputed to have lived next door. Moreover, Deptford is riddled with tunnels, one of which ends at number 34. They were built under the instructions of the sea-captains, who were fed up with their booty being stolen on their way back home. Did Lady Hamilton and Captain Nelson use the tunnels to rendezvous? Fiction or reality, there's no denying that Albury Street is full of charm. Fans of J.K. Rowling will recognise it as Robin's home, in book four of the *Cormoran Strike* series.

Address Anchor Iron Wharf, London, SE10 9GL | Getting there Bus 129, 177, 180 or 286 to Marlton Street, then walk along the river, taking a right at Trafalgar Tavern; train to Maze Hill; DLR to Greenwich, then a 10-minute walk | Tip To prolong the visit, locate the steps opposite Midpoint Restaurant; these aren't obvious but will take you beneath the jetty to a small beach. But take care: the descent is always slippery!

3 — Angerstein Foot Crossing
Stop, Look, Listen

This unassuming foot crossing, reached via a discreet alleyway between houses, may be unique in London. No wonder that in 2019, when threatened with closure, it became a hot topic. True, it's a very convenient short-cut and widely used by local commuters to get to Westcombe Park station, but it's also a symbol of our industrial past.

John Julius Angerstein was a London businessman born in St. Petersburg, Russia. There is speculation that he was of royal ancestry, but we'll never know. The fact remains that he arrived in London aged 15, and started a career in finance, later working for Lloyd's Bank as an underwriter. In 1774, he invested in land in the area now known as Westcombe Park and Greenwich Peninsula, hoping for good returns. This was a shrewd if not long-term investment. Almost a century on, in 1849, once the link between London and the North Kent Railway was completed, it paid off.

A railway line was needed to connect the mainline to the river to transport heavy goods. It was decided that the track would run across Angerstein's land. People couldn't travel the line, only heavy materials from sand to steel and everything in between were transported on the Angerstein narrow gauge railway. As it was a short and private line, building it was straightforward, and soon goods were on their way. The only problem came with getting livestock across. Farmworkers called for a right of way for their stock to cross safely; the problem was solved with the Angerstein Foot Crossing.

By 1950, the track terminal at Angerstein Wharf was considered too small to handle modern shipping, but it's still useful for aggregate and other movements of stock. The single-track line is still operational, albeit with fewer trains running. Trainspotters take note: the foot crossing is the only place from which to get an excellent view of this historical railway line.

Address 32 Farmdale Road, London, SE10 0LS | Getting there Train to Westcombe Park, go to the car park at the rear, and take the bridge over the A2; bus 108, 286, 335 or 422 to Westerdale Road; it's a little easier from the other side of the footpath: take the alley next to 132 Fairthorn Street | Tip One of the curios of the railway line between Greenwich and Woolwich is the fact that it still has a level crossing at the lower end of Charlton Lane, to allow over 300 trains a day to pass. This is the only level crossing left in Inner London, so the area has not one but two treats for train fans.

4 Avery Hill Park

The pleasure-dome of the 'Nitrate King'

While not South London's, or even Greenwich's, most beguiling corner, nor even its most interesting park, the wide open spaces of Avery Hill Park hide one of the borough's hidden treasures – the second-largest glasshouse in the country. It's now part of the Greenwich University campus, and was once part of the 600-acre estate of the 19th-century businessman John Thomas North, a Yorkshireman who retired here after making his fortune in Chile.

North was one of the most successful entrepreneurs of his day, a businessman and adventurer who was sent to Chile in his youth to oversee the manufacture of machinery. He got lucky when he took control of the nitrates industry there, establishing a monopoly in the export of saltpetre for fertiliser, and becoming hugely wealthy in the process. He made a lot of people in Chile rich too, and contributed to the rise of the town of Iquique.

North returned to the UK and built the house of his dreams, Avery Hill House, in 1890: photographs show a sumptuous balustraded mansion with a moustachioed North standing proudly outside. He entertained lavishly, and hunted with the Prince of Wales among others, but lived here for only a few years, until his sudden death in 1896. The house was later sold, and the only traces of North's pleasure-dome that remain are a series of formal gardens, and the glasshouses he constructed to enjoy the views over what must, in its day, have been a sumptuous country estate.

The glasshouse is a magnificent building, in the process of being rescued from dereliction by the university. It is once again full of palms, cacti and desert plants in its main hall. One wing remains in a state of disrepair, but the other is a soothing space complete with fountain, statue and benches for visitors to enjoy it all – a proper Winter Garden, in fact, and reason enough alone for a trip to Avery Hill.

Address Bexley Road, London, SE9 2EU | Getting there Train to Falconwood, then a 15-minute walk; bus 132 or 286 stop right outside | Hours Always open | Tip Avery Hill Park is on the fabulous 'Green Chain Walk', an 82km route through south-east London that runs through part of what would have been North's vast estate. Divided into 11 sections, Avery Hill Park is on the Shepherdleas Wood to Middle Park section of the Walk. Tarn Bird Sanctuary (see ch. 94) is a short walk away in one direction, and Oxleas Woods (see ch. 57) in the other.

5 — Blackheath
Wide-open spaces right outside Greenwich Park

Split across the border of Lewisham and Greenwich boroughs, Blackheath's open spaces are right outside Greenwich Park, and contribute to the leafy ambience of this desirable part of south-east London. Greenwich officially ends with the busy artery of Shooter's Hill, which traverses the Heath on its way to Deptford and Old Kent Road. But there's plenty to see on the Greenwich side – not least the Ranger's House (see ch. 72), which faces the residential slopes on the western side of the park walls, just along from General Wolfe's childhood home, McCartney House. It's a lovely spot, overlooking some of Greenwich's grandest and most historic houses. But it wasn't always peaceful.

It was here that Wat Tyler rallied his men before their assault on London during the Peasant's Revolt in 1381, and a plaque by the park's main entrance commemorates the Cornish rebels who met here in 1497, before being defeated at the battle of Deptford Bridge. It's a myth, however, that Blackheath is so named because many victims of the Black Death were buried here; it is in fact more likely derived from 'Blachheldefeld', which simply means 'Dark Heath'. Easy to imagine that this might have been an appropriate name for this wide, treeless expanse on a plateau above the Thames flood plain.

On the other side of the park, across Maze Hill, which leads down past John Vanbrugh's eccentric castle (see ch. 103), lie a series of gravel pits. Now mostly overgrown with trees and gorse, these are known locally as 'The Dips'. You can stroll through here from the park, and then perhaps amble through the various paths and private roads on the far side. One of these, Angerstein Lane, is named after a local founder of Lloyds of London and art collector whose collection formed the basis of the National Gallery when it opened in the 1820s. He built and lived in Woodlands House, which still stands in nearby Westcombe Park (see ch. 3 for more about Angerstein).

Address Blackheath, SE3 | Getting there Train to Maze Hill, Westcombe Park or Blackheath; bus 53 or 54 | Hours Always open | Tip Stick around and explore one of Blackheath's two commercial centres: 'Blackheath Standard', a collection of shops, cafés and restaurants around the nearby 'Royal Standard' pub, or 'Blackheath Village', one of London's most delightful 'villages' that's just a five-minute stroll across the heath, also offering numerous pubs, restaurants, shops and cafés.

6 __ Blue Cross Pet Cemetery

When the time comes to say goodbye to beloved pets

The Old Blue Cross Pet Cemetery on Shooters Hill is hidden away down a small alleyway, between the Lido (see ch. 11) and a block of flats. It is a little oasis of calm. Although pet cemeteries are growing in popularity, there are only a few such sites around London. But, in this small public park, much-loved cats, dogs and even a hamster have been laid to rest since 1906. This unusual cemetery is being restored by a group of dedicated volunteers, many of whom are local dog owners. They are cleaning up poignant tiny graves, planting flowers, even going as far as installing power lines.

Little is known about the early history of the place as most records were lost in a fire. At the start of the 20th century, there were private kennels nearby, run by a veterinary army officer. In 1909, Huskies from Ernest Shackleton's Arctic Expedition spent their quarantine here. The site also played an important role in World War I. By then, the Blue Cross had acquired the kennels, and army personnel could safely leave their pets here while they served their country. When the time came, the animals were laid to rest. There are 240 graves, the earliest dated 1906 for a dog called Boyce. Most headstones no longer stand but lay flat among the paving stones. In many ways these pets were the lucky ones, unlike the 2.9 million dogs and cats put to sleep in 1939 by order of the government, to spare them the horrors of war. An unimaginable situation today, when pets are treated like internet superstars.

Pets are no longer buried here, however, as interments stopped in the 1940s, replaced by memorial plaques for much-loved companions. Stories behind the names are remarkable, such as that of Bonzo Tabner who lived in Greenwich during World War II. The dog must have lost its name tag, as it was recently recovered by well-known local mudlark Nicola White (see ch. 49). Read his story on the wall by the entrance of the cemetery.

Address The Old Blue Cross Pet Cemetery, Shooters Hill Road, London, SE18 4LX, www.oldbluecrosspetcemetery.org.uk | **Getting there** Take the footpath marked by a blue sign, opposite the Shooters Hill's pub the Fox under the Hill, where there's a round blue plaque indicating the entrance of the site; bus 89 or 486 to Hornfair Park and Lido | **Hours** Unrestricted | **Tip** The borough, with its many green spaces, is dog-friendly. A few pubs go out of their way to welcome dogs and their owners, offering treats and water bowls. The Hare & Billet, SE3 0QJ, is one of them.

Roundel designed and created by
Adrian Brough
www.adrianbroughpottery.co.uk

Remembering Wartime Pets

In memory of cats and dogs and all animal companions of this country who lost their lives or otherwise suffered in the Second World War. More than two million died, most of them early in conflict, not as a result of enemy action but when the despairing owners acted on tragically misguided official advice to have their pets put down. New dangers faced survivors – who went on to make their own remarkable contribution, as was said at the war's end:
'Dogs have dug into wrecked homes looking for their owners. Cats have mewed for days outside the piles of rubble, telling rescuers their owners are buried there.
Animals have quietened distressed children.
Yet when the history of the war is written these things will not be recorded.' Now they are.
Clare and Christy Campbell
Authors of "Bonzo's War" August 2019

Discovering Bonzo

In June 2018 Thames mudlark Nicola White found a corroded tag from a dog collar on the Thames beach at Greenwich bearing the name "Bonzo Tabner". Not only did she discover he was a much-loved pet to a family in Greenwich during World War II, but she also discovered the book "Bonzo's War" which detailed the fate of over two million pets during the war.
Moved by the story, Nicola contacted the authors of "Bonzo's War" and launched a fundraising campaign to purchase a permanent memorial in memory of these pets.
The River Thames reveals many stories from the past and this is one of the most poignant.
May the love and devotion of "Bonzo Tabner", and the pets of World War II never be forgotten
Nicola White August 2019

7 Caird Library and Archive

The world's largest maritime library and archive

Greenwich's Maritime Museum is a focus for research into maritime matters, and nowhere is this truer than the Caird Library, tucked away in the museum's Sammy Ofer wing. This is home to around 150,000 volumes, encompassing ancient and rare books, periodicals and pamphlets. Named after Sir James Caird, the sponsor of Shackleton's ill-fated Antarctic expedition, and the eponymous lifeboat used on the monumental journey to South Georgia during 1916, it has been open since 1937, and is home to over 80,000 maps and charts, some of which date back as far as the 15th century. It is, in short, a dream destination for anyone remotely interested in maritime history, books or maps.

Unlike many other specialist London collections, you don't need to be an academic to access its treasures – indeed you can view the contemporary books, magazines and journals on the open shelves at no cost, simply by signing up for a day pass. Behind here, however, lie the real treasures, for which a full library card is needed (although anyone can obtain one of these). There is, for example, the medical almanac from *The Bounty*, full of good advice for sailors on how to stay healthy, gruesome guides to naval surgery from the early 19th century, with plentiful illustrations and tips on amputation, and folios relating to the Armada. There are also rare gems such as the country's premier collection of Nelson-related books, letters and manuscripts, Franklin's last handwritten message from the ill-fated Northwest Passage expedition, and papers, photos and ephemera rescued from the *Titanic*.

Many people spend days in the Caird Library researching their seafaring ancestors, but it's worth popping in even for a short visit. It's a haven of peace compared with the rest of the museum, and throughout the year there are regular exhibitions that are free to all. The Caird Library and Archive is certainly one of the most compelling of Greenwich's lesser-known attractions.

Address National Maritime Museum, Romney Road, London, SE10 9NF | Getting there Train to Greenwich or Maze Hill; DLR to Cutty Sark; bus 129, 177, 180, 188, 199, 286 or 386 to Greenwich town centre | Hours Daily 10am–5pm | Tip Supplement your trip to the library by investing in a map, chart or ship's plan, either at the museum which prints copies of its own ship's plans to order, or across the road at the Warwick Leadlay Gallery, tucked away in the alley off the market. They sell all sorts of plans and charts, both originals and reprints, naturally with an emphasis on Greenwich, but with plenty more besides.

8_ Caradoc Street
Pretty as a picture, this street is a legend

South East London is often stereotyped as being rough with pockets of respectability such as Greenwich. That said, Greenwich is a place of two halves: broadly-speaking, the west is gentrified, while the east is gritty. Although located in a conservation zone, East Greenwich largely fails to appear on tourists' radar. The area consists of a maze of small streets leading to the Thames, and this is where you'll find Caradoc Street, in a charming and characterful enclave.

This sweet little street is lined by rows of two-up, two-down terraced houses, built for dock workers and their families in London's yellow brick stock. They all look very similar, but while some are Georgian, others are much older, having escaped the ravages of the Blitz. They make the street unique, and a prime site popular with film and music video makers. For example, it features in the official video for Oasis' single, '*The Importance of Being Idle*'.

The street was also made famous by its appearance in two feature films relating to the life and exploits of London's notorious Kray twins. The Krays' famous gang 'The Firm' terrorised London in the 1960s, the motto of Kray twins Reginald and Ronnie being, 'Always shoot to kill, dead men cannot grass'. Number 32 Caradoc Street provided the set for The Krays' family home 'Fortress Valance'. By coincidence, number 32 also appears in the second film about the brothers, 2015's *Legend*. This time, the house was the family home of Reggie's first wife, Frances Shea. Their marriage lasted 18 months, culminating in Frances' tragic suicide, at the age of 23. In real life, the Krays were from Bethnal Green, a little further east, but their main rival gang, the Richardsons, whose outfit went under the apt name of 'The Torture Gang', operated in this area. With these gangster-ridden days gone, Caradoc is now a lovely, well maintained street with flower boxes in the windows.

Address Caradoc Street, London, SE10 9AG | Getting there Tube to North Greenwich (Jubilee Line), then bus 188 or 422 to King William; train to Maze Hill | Tip Greenwich can lay claim to being one of the most popular film locations in the world: take a walk in the university grounds, and you'll soon be transported to the set of *Pirates of the Caribbean*, *The Queen*, and many more.

9 Casbah Records
Simply the best

Whether or not this independent shop was named after *Rock the Casbah*, the hit song by The Clash, Casbah Records is aptly named: the store's racks are crammed full of new and vintage vinyl, CDs, DVDs, tapes, as well as comics, and more. Owner/manager Graham Davis and the rest of the Casbah's team give the venue a unique atmosphere. No two ways about it, this shop is a destination, and sits perfectly among Greenwich's other shops, which are mainly antiquarian or second-hand establishments. The result is a town centre environment that's unique to south-east London.

The Davis brothers' adventure started in the mid-1980s, when they had a stall on Greenwich market. There was a brief interlude in 1994 that involved a vehicle akin to a library bus, with which they toured the county's music festivals with their wares, but eventually the business was taken indoors at the shop's current location.

In a world of record collectors which is mostly male-dominated, it's refreshing to see that the staff behind the counter at Casbah Records are mostly young, creative, female students from the nearby universities. They advise clients, promote new stock, and manage the shop's social media channels. And any customers looking for a rare find may be rewarded: the shop once sold a first pressing of *Led Zeppelin 1* with turquoise lettering on the front for £1,500.

With more than 40 years in the trade, Graham Davis knows all the best places where to source his stock. Acquisitions are made with the general public in mind, but he never forgets to tailor his purchases towards the tastes of his regular customers. On Record Store Day, the one day of the year when over 200 independent record shops across the UK celebrate their unique culture, people queue up outside Casbah Records from midnight to get their hands on limited editions. That's the reward for being the best in town.

Address 320-322 Creek Road, London, SE10 9SW, +44 (0)20 8858 1964, www.casbahrecords.co.uk | Getting there DLR to Cutty Sark; train to Greenwich; boat, MBNA Thames Clippers depart from all major London piers every 20 minutes; bus 53, 54, 129, 177, 180, 188, 199, 202, 286, 380, 386 or N1 to Cutty Sark | Hours Mon 11.30am–6pm, Tue–Fri 10.30am–6pm, Sat & Sun 10.30am–6.30pm | Tip Among the numerous music venues it would be easy to miss Mycenae House – a community hub in a historic building offering live music events (90 Mycenae Road, www.mycenaehouse.co.uk).

10_ Charlton House
London's finest Jacobean Mansion – with mulberries

Nothing quite prepares you for your first view of this Jacobean mansion, whose magnificent frontage is a contrast to its immediate surroundings. Completed in 1612, it's a remarkable remnant of a time when Charlton was a genteel Kentish village overlooking the Thames beyond London. Built as the residence of Adam Newton, tutor to the son of James I, it was designed by architect John Thorpe, who is believed to have worked on the Royal Palace in Greenwich. While the interior isn't as well preserved as the mostly excellent exterior, access is easy, and you can stroll in to examine what's left of the house's fine ceilings and carved fireplaces, along with the Stuart coat of arms and monogram of James I – that is, if you're prepared to risk the attentions of the house's many ghosts!

Be sure to observe the contemporaneous Summer House on the main road, long thought to be an early work of Inigo Jones – despite being used for years as a public toilet! – now about to undergo major restoration. The spreading mulberry tree beside it is believed to be the oldest in the country, planted in 1608 on the orders of James, as part of his aim to plant 10,000 mulberry trees to stimulate the domestic silk industry (silkworms love mulberries). The tree still fruits every year, its mulberries sometimes finding their way into the dishes served in the house's Tea Room, which offers a variety of refreshments.

You can also visit the formal walled gardens, which include a couple of borders that must once have been magnificent but are now a little neglected. Beyond, however, a short stretch of a Ha-Ha – a ditch commonly dug in the 18th century to act as a barrier between formal gardens and grazed parkland without spoiling the view – testifies to the former grandeur of the estate. As John Evelyn wrote, the prospect from Charlton House was 'one of the most noble in the world, for city, river, ships, meadows, hills, woods and all other amenities'.

Address Charlton House, Charlton Road, London, SE7 8RE, +44 (0)20 8856 3951, www.greenwichheritage.org/visit/charlton-house | Getting there Bus 53, 54, 380, 422 or 486 to Charlton Village; train to Charlton and a 10-minute uphill walk | Hours Mon–Fri 9am–5pm | Tip Behind the house, Charlton Park was created out of the rest of the house's extensive grounds, and is a pleasant way to reach the main sights of Woolwich and its common a little way beyond.

11 Charlton Lido

Splish! Splash!

Lye-doh or Lee-doh, whichever way you pronounce it, lidos are rare enough that people take notice when there's one nearby. Given the British weather, this is the kind of facility the municipalities aren't always keen to invest in. This contrasts with the 1930s, when the infatuation with open-air pools was at its height, and a total of 169 lidos were built across the country.

Charlton Lido was the last open-air swimming pool to be built in London. Nowadays, there are around 100 of them left, many of which are closed during the winter. In Charlton, the 50-metre Olympic-sized heated pool can be enjoyed throughout the year, which probably explains the close-knit community of regular swimmers. In 2019, a crowd gathered to celebrate the 80th anniversary of the pool's opening. Attendees included Olympic gold medallist Duncan Goodhew MBE, and local swimmer Tom Gregory. Tom grew up on a nearby estate, and was the youngest person ever to swim across the English Channel, taking 11 hours and 54 minutes to do so, shortly before his 12th birthday.

The story of Charlton Lido hasn't been plain sailing, however. It opened at the start of World War II, soon after it was requisitioned as a fire emergency water supply. It reopened to the public in 1946, and remained in use until the end of 1989, at which point public funding dried up. There followed some 13 years of on-and-off access until 2012, when it was saved from dereliction and underwent full refurbishment. Now it looks dazzling, with its Roman-style brick courtyard walls, poolside changing cubicles and sun-loungers. There are also various fitness facilities, including exercise bikes.

Adjacent to the Lido is a large park with formal gardens, and areas for different sporting activities, such as a BMX track and basketball court. And in case you're wondering, the Cambridge English Pronouncing Dictionary advocates *Lee-doh*.

Address Charlton Lido, Hornfair Park, Shooters Hill Road, London, SE18 4LX, www.better.org.uk/leisure-centre/london/greenwich/charlton-lido | Getting there Bus 53, 89, 178 or 386; train to Charlton and walk, or to Lewisham and bus 21 | Hours Times vary throughout the year, but summer is usually Mon–Fri 6.30am–8pm, Sat & Sun 9am–5pm; book online and check the pool timetable before visiting | Tip Other water sports include kayaking in Greenwich with London Kayak Company (+44 (0)7741 205 515, www.londonkayakcompany.com).

12 Charlton Village

A proper village where you least expect one!

Who would have thought that Charlton had a village? For most people, this working-class neighbourhood, representing the meat in the sandwich between the more illustrious suburbs of Greenwich and Woolwich, is forever associated with the few ups and multiple downs of its famous football team, Charlton Athletic (see ch.102).

The historic heart of Charlton is, however, a classic village high street, dating back some 300 years to when it formed the centre of Charlton-next-Woolwich – 'a village', according to Daniel Defoe, 'famous for the yearly collected rabble of mad-people, at Horn Fair; the rudeness of which … ought to be suppressed'. Defoe's observation could be considered a harsh one, but Charlton's annual Horn Fair was certainly a raucous event, at which people got so drunk and rowdy that it was banned altogether in the 1870s. It was revived in a more anodyne form in 2009, with a parade starting at Rotherhithe, and finishing at the eponymous park just a step away from Charlton's Village.

Meanwhile, Charlton's real heritage is manifested in the Jacobean magnificence of Charlton House (see ch. 10), whose grounds extend to Charlton Park behind, and, almost opposite, dinky 17th-century St Luke's, which has the look and feel of a proper village church. A replacement of a far more ancient building, it's a cosy little church whose tower was once used as a point of navigation for ships on the Thames. More importantly, its churchyard is the last resting place of one Spencer Perceval, the only British prime minister to have been assassinated. He suffered numerous crises during his term in office from 1809 to 1812, most notably the Napoleonic Wars and the Luddite Revolt, and was finally shot dead in the House of Commons by a Liverpool merchant. It's an incident that's hardly known about, least of all by Charlton locals, who would be surprised to learn they had a prime minister in their midst!

Address The Village, London, SE7 8UG | Getting there Bus 53, 54, 380 or 422 | Hours Always open | Tip Take the weight off your feet at one of the village's excellent watering holes – the Grade II-listed Bugle Horn opposite the church, or the very convivial White Swan further along the road.

13 The Cheeseboard

Best meals are made of cheese

Royal Hill is known for its variety of fine food shops, such as The Creaky Shed, Drings the butcher, and Ellis and Jones the fishmonger. But of particular interest is The Cheeseboard – an artisan cheese shop that's been in business on the same premises since 1984.

The Cheeseboard's popularity has increased in recent years, judging by the length of the queues in the shop, which sometimes spill out onto the pavement. The secret of its success? 150 British and International cheeses, all attractively displayed and clearly labelled, and served by friendly and knowledgeable staff. Buying fine cheese can often be intimidating: creating the perfect cheeseboard is no easy task! Even picking a single cheese can be tricky. But at The Cheeseboard the process is made easy as the staff give you their full attention, helping you choose from a variety of textures and flavours to get just the right product. You can even try before you buy. When it comes to cheese the French get all the glory, and the shop's best-seller is a version of Comté matured for 24-30 months using a traditional Jurassian method. But it turns out that Scandinavians make a popular soft, sweet cheese which name is already a mouthful: Gjetost.

Like most good cheese shops, The Cheeseboard offers vegetarian friendly alternatives such as Old Winchester and a wide range of complementary products, most of which are locally produced: bread, pickles, wine and beer to name but a few. Before you know it, you'll have purchased enough for an entire meal of delicacies. There are even confections for special occasions, such as cheese wedding cakes. Here, each is named after a Greenwich pub and features a selection of cheeses arranged over several tiers. The origins of such towers are unknown, but could have started with Queen Victoria's wedding, when she and Prince Albert received a 1,000lb (453kg) Cheddar-style cheese as a gift – now that's a cheese fit for a queen!

VACHE qui RIT

VACHERIN
MONT d'OR
£3.60

St. JUDE
£7.95
SUFFOLK

ELRICK
LOG
£11=
SCOTLAND

SINODUN
HILL
£11.95
each

MARMITE
CHEESE STRAWS
£1.50

Address The Cheeseboard, 26 Royal Hill, London, SE10 8RT, +44 (0)20 8305 0401, www.cheese-board.co.uk | **Getting there** Bus 177, 180 or 188; train or DLR to Greenwich | **Hours** Mon–Wed 9am–9pm, Thu 9am–1pm, Fri 9am–5.30pm, Sat 9am–5pm | **Tip** Nearby on Burney Road is an unusual plaque depicting a man driving a milk truck. It reads *Doug Mullins 1932–1991, Master Dairyman, born over the shop at this site.* For Doug's funeral the streets were lined with people, and the wreath on the hearse was milk bottle shaped.

Tomme de
Chèvre Georgian
£4.30

CRÈME
CHÈVRE

MONTE
ENEBRO

14 Crossness Engines
Engineering solution to London's 'Great Stink'

In the early 19th century, London wasn't a very wholesome place. The Thames was used as the city's main sewer, and as a result several major cholera outbreaks, in 1831, 1848 and 1853, killed many thousands of people. Finally, the so-called 'Great Stink' of 1858, when warm weather and raw sewage combined to produce a foul and pervasive stench, motivated the authorities to invest in a proper sewerage system.

Enter Joseph Bazalgette, an engineer and friend of Isambard Kingdom Brunel who headed up London's Board of Works and had a plan for a series of tunnels to collect sewage and divert it into a number of larger tunnels. These would carry it east along the river to pumping stations, where it could be sent out to sea. He enclosed these under the Albert, Victoria and Chelsea Embankments, and improved the city's aroma forever.

Designed by architect Charles Driver, Crossness was the scheme's first pumping station, located at the end of the so-called Southern Outfall sewer in the Erith Marshes, now Thamesmead. They basically pumped the sewage into a 25-million-gallon underground reservoir (still in use), then released it into the river on the ebbing tide. Like its sister station on the north side of the river in Stratford, the building is a true Victorian gem. There are rows of Romanesque arches on the outside, while inside its original four steam engines are still in place, with their enormous flywheels and the intricate, colourful ironwork of its main octagonal hall.

The original Crossness works fell into disrepair after being replaced by a more modern facility in the 1950s, but it's since been beautifully restored and is now open to the public once a month, with regular Open Days when the machinery is brought into life. There's still a bit of whiff in the air, for sure, but it is truly one of south-east London's most unusual and impressive sights.

Address Bazalgette Way, London, SE2 9AQ | Getting there Train to Abbey Wood, then a 20-minute walk | Hours Open days around once a month | Tip There's lots of green space around Crossness: follow a path to the river, enjoy a picnic by the lake in Southmere Park, or follow the Ridgeway path – a 3.5-mile footpath that follows the route of the Southern Outfall sewer back to Plumstead.

15 _Cutty Sark_
The phoenix of the seas

Cutty Sark needs no introduction: she has been synonymous with Greenwich ever since she was put in dry dock in 1954, following 80 years at sea. She's the last surviving tea clipper on the planet. Her longevity is remarkable, and the result of a lot of good luck offsetting considerable misfortune and adversity.

Built in 1869 for the great China Tea Races, the vessel wasn't expected to last much more than 30 years; yet, 150 years later, she still delights us. On a number of occasions, the ship was nearly lost, but every time she rose again like a phoenix of the sea. In 1922, flying the Portuguese flag, she was nearly destroyed after being badly damaged in a storm, only to be spotted by a 'fan' – a retired sea captain who returned her to the UK. Her coming to Greenwich was another piece of good fortune. The site had been reserved for Battle of Trafalgar survivor HMS _Implacable,_ but in 1949 the veteran ship was scuttled. Then, when in 2007 a fire broke out during restoration work, it was fortunate that 90% of the original fabric had already been removed.

Climb aboard to appreciate the crew's living conditions. Contrary to popular belief, if the bunks seem small, this isn't because people were smaller then than they are today: the tightness of the bunk beds is purely practical, stopping sailors rolling with the swell.

Among her many treasures, it's easy to spot Nannie the Witch, holding a horse's tail and scantily clad in her nightie, also called a cutty sark. The Long John Silver Collection is one of the largest collections of figureheads in the world, but the most glorious object is a masthead vane. This vane, in the shape of Nannie's cutty sark, was presented to the ship by her owner in 1886, on the occasion of her record passage: 73 days from Sydney to London. A gilded replica glitters on the 150ft main mast, while the battle-worn original can be admired on the tween deck.

Address King William Walk, London, SE10 9HT, +44 (0)20 8858 4422, www.rmg.co.uk/cutty-sark | Getting there DLR to Cutty Sark; train to Greenwich; boat, MBNA Thames Clippers depart from all major London piers every 20 minutes; bus 53, 54, 129, 177, 180, 188, 199, 202, 286, 380, 386 or N1 to Cutty Sark | Hours Access all-year round; go aboard daily 10.30am–4pm | Tip *Gloriana*, The Queen's Rowbarge, used for her Diamond Jubilee in 2012, has been provided with a boathouse and will soon dock at Morden Wharf on Greenwich Peninsula.

16 Davy's Wine Lodge

A fascinating building and a Greenwich institution

One of Greenwich's most famous names is Lovibond, a local brewing family dating from the 19th and 20th centuries. Their name lives on in the original brewery building on Greenwich South Street, which they built on land purchased from the nearby railway in 1859. They stopped brewing at the end of the 1950s, and turned the building into a wine warehouse. Since 1971 this has been home to another Greenwich institution: Davy's Wine Lodge.

Davy's has operated in London since 1870, and was a pioneer of the 1970s wine bar craze, when fourth-generation chairman, John Davy, launched the Boot & Flogger in Southwark, and generally helped nurture the UK's love affair with wine. Now run by John's son James, Davy's is a substantial wine distribution business, supplying wine merchants, hotels and restaurants all over the country, and makes good use of the substantial maze of Victorian cellars that run beneath the building. With the company's establishment in Greenwich, Davy's Wine Vaults is your best chance to experience this fascinating, labyrinthine old building first-hand.

Davy's is one of the most unusual eateries in the area – sensitively updated while retaining the classic essence of the original Victorian structure. The sloping floor was designed to facilitate the easy rolling of barrels from the street, and the building is crammed full of wine paraphernalia, with a curio around every corner: the bar is made from old port barrels, there are wine presses and bottle-corkers, coopers' tools and old crates, alongside cuttings and sepia photos of the Davy family. There's even a stuffed albatross tucked away in one corner! Open every day for lunch and dinner, Davy's serves excellent Modern British food, with a predictably impressive wine list. And if you find something you like, you can buy it next door in Davy's Wine Shop – which is a wine browser's paradise.

Address 161 Greenwich High Road, London, SE10 8JA, +44 (0)20 7407 9670, www.davy.co.uk | Getting there Train or DLR to Greenwich; bus 177, 180, 199 or 386 | Hours Daily, usually until 11.30pm; open for breakfast at weekends | Tip If you want to learn more about wine then join one of Davy's' evening wine courses and 'tutored tastings'.

17 __Deptford Creek

No wading boots needed to read this page

As the city of London grew throughout history, the streams and small rivers feeding the Thames represented obstacles to the city's development, and so they were buried. Today, in many parts of London, including Greenwich, you could be standing near one of the 22 Thames tributaries without realising it. These include rivers such as The Fleet, which gave its name to Fleet Street, or The Brooks, as in Kidbrooke. They are collectively known as 'London's Lost Rivers', and have a fascinating history. But not all are hidden: the Ravensbourne has its own tributary, The Quaggy – affectionately called Little Quaggy – which resurfaces now and then, sometimes in odd places such as a garden, but always providing excitement and a sense of wonder. The Ravensbourne passes from Caesar's Well in Keston to Deptford, where it enters the Thames. Being a fast-flowing river, its power was harnessed by several water mills from the Norman times through to the Victorian era, with 15 in operation between Deptford Creek and Lewisham.

There are a few ways to get close to the Ravensbourne, but the most exciting is to walk on the river bed. Evidently, this is not something to do on your own: you'll need a guide, walking poles, and a pair of wading boots – all of which can be provided by Creekside Discovery Centre for participants in its low-tide walks, led by conservationists. There's nothing like observing tiny shrimps, Chinese Mitten Crabs, leeches, and the surrounding flora to become aware of our impact on the environment.

Deptford continues to change, with high-rises encroaching rapidly. As a result, Sand Martins and the people of the long-established boating community are fighting for survival in the area. Until now, a range of vessels have moored under the DLR. You'd have to be aware of their existence to spot them, but some have called Deptford Creek home for the past 30 years.

Address Creekside Discovery Centre, 14 Creekside, London, SE8 4SA, +44 (0)20 8692 9922, www.creeksidecentre.co.uk | Getting there Bus 177, 188 or 199 to H MacMillan Students Village; DLR to Deptford Bridge | Tip Over the years five bridges have been built across the Creek. Ha'penny Hatch footbridge is an industrial landmark, opened in 2002 on the site of an old toll bridge – costing half a penny to cross – which closed in the 1920s. It's worth the stroll, as the iron structure is a vertical lifting bridge, and quite a sight.

18 Deptford High Street

Historic yet misunderstood neighbourhood

Named after the so-called 'deep ford' of the Ravensbourne river, a tributary of the Thames which joins the main river at Deptford Creek, in the 16th century Deptford was London's major military dockyard. Home to the nation's ships, shipbuilders and the stars of its navy, it was here that Sir Francis Drake was knighted by Elizabeth I, where Captain James Cooke left on his third and final voyage aboard the *Resolution* and where Peter the Great came from Russia to study shipbuilding in the 18th century.

Nowadays, it's a tough inner-city neighbourhood whose gentrification has been long predicted but never quite happened, with Deptford's hipsters and students and multicultural working-class populations happily co-existing. This is nowhere truer than on the main drag, Deptford High Street, where the market holds sway as far as the beached anchor at the junction of Deptford Broadway – a reminder of the district's seafaring roots. The market is a long-running, raucous affair, mainly comprising stalls selling cheap clothes, electrical goods, phone cases and ersatz designer bags, behind which an abundance of grocery stores do a roaring trade in fresh veg, salt-fish and other West Indian delights. Nearby Douglas Way is home to a bric-a-brac market, while the revamped square around the train station, and the railway arches either side, offer a more hipsterish ambience, with cool coffee shops, the odd craft brewery, and outside tables for al fresco socialising.

The non-pedestrianised part of the high street continues past vintage and new clothes outlets, tattoo studios, Vietnamese restaurants and the long-standing local landmark of Manze's Pie & Mash (see ch. 44) to Creek Road. Beyond this, Deptford's most famous murder victim, Christopher Marlowe, lies buried in the churchyard of St Nicholas – just look for the skull and crossbones on the gate (see ch. 91)!

Address High Street, London, SE8 3PR | Getting there Train to Deptford; DLR to Deptford Bridge; various buses to Deptford Broadway or Creek Road | Hours Market Wed, Fri & Sat 9am–5pm | Tip Look in on the Albany Theatre just off the high street on Douglas Way, a 1980s upgrade of the original Albany Empire, which used to be around the corner on Creek Road, and once hosted many famous bands, including local boys Squeeze and Dire Straits.

19 Diamond Terrace and Mines

Put the shovel away, no diamonds here

Diamond Terrace is situated in an exclusive residential area. At first, the private road looks like a back alley bordered by few garages – but don't be fooled: this is a desirable location with several splendid, Grade II-listed houses. The best examples are three-storey family homes with special architectural features, such as delightful wrought iron balconies, fancy latticed spandrels, and friezes. One house in this little enclave hides one of the best-kept subterranean secrets in Greenwich: an intriguing mine! The existing tunnels leading to disused mines are some of the last remains of an extensive network. None are yet open to the public, which makes what lies beneath these Georgian houses even more fascinating. The few people who have gained access to the tunnels in the past recorded portraits of Shirley Temple and Mussolini carved in the walls. They also noticed graffiti from World War II, as the tunnels were used as air-raid shelters. Other scribbles refer to when the passages led to working mines. Sand mines are a significant part of Greenwich's industrial heritage, but little is known about their purpose. The sand was too coarse for glass making, for example, but could have been used for sanding floors – perhaps even the wooden floors of the grand houses in Diamond Terrace.

Beautiful properties call for beautiful views. Stroll out of Diamond Terrace to The Point, a nearby vista with one of the best London panoramas. On a clear day it's possible to see all the way to St Paul's, and beyond as far as Essex. In contrast to the top of the park, around General Wolfe's statue, The Point is hardly ever busy – apart from New Year's Eve, when locals congregate to toast the future. At any other time, without crowds wielding selfie-sticks, you can simply sit on a bench and enjoy a romantic moment. Diamonds not included!

Address Diamond Terrace, London, SE10 8QN; this is a private road so please respect residents' privacy | Getting there Train to Greenwich; bus 177 or 180 to Marlton Street; DLR or boat to Cutty Sark; all are followed by a five-minute walk to Royal Hill, then walk from Royal Hill to Point Hill; Diamond Terrace is second on the left | Tip Among the tunnels under the park the conduits are much talked-about, but little is known about them. Built to carry water, they're now sealed up, but it's still possible to see two covered entrances at the foot of the park – they look like little houses.

20__The Dog and Bell
Thirsty? A traditional pub worth visiting

The good old Dog and Bell, a Great British boozer, one of these rare locals that corporations spend millions trying to emulate without success. You wouldn't know the place existed unless you'd stumbled upon it or been taken there. It's well-hidden, despite its jolly red façade, with its windows dressed for every regional or national occasion. Located in a cul-de-sac, there are barrel-tables, benches and planters at the front, and a small garden at the rear.

The Dog and Bell is all about beer. In fact it's an oasis of real ales. A few years ago there were concerns when publican Charles Gallagher and his wife Eileen stepped back after over three decades behind the bar. They had ensured that the pub's atmosphere remained simple and focussed on a traditional welcome. To the locals' relief another Irishman took over – Seamus O'Neill, who is building upon the Gallaghers' firm foundations. Beer is still the main focus. While the pub's anchor beer is Fuller's London Pride, there are eight changing guest beers, in addition to another six new pumps for craft beers. There's also a large selection of bottled Belgian beers. Punters can also find cider and one of London's largest collections of Irish Whiskey, meaning there's something for all tastes.

Once a year people gather for the pub's annual famous Pickle Festival, one of the few celebrations of its kind in existence. It's a fun night, when locals enter their home-made preserves, and the crowd, after much tasting, decide on the winners. Competition is fierce, but that doesn't stop contestants having a good time and a knees-up in Prince Street. Since opening in 1741, the pub changed its name briefly to The Royal Marine, a salute to the Commando Force stationed in the Royal Dockyard, although even then locals continued to refer to the pub as The Dog and Bell. Why not pay a visit and enjoy a drink in this welcoming establishment.

Address 116 Prince Street, London, SE8 3JD, +44 (0)20 8692 5664 | Getting there The pub is off Watergate Street; DLR to Deptford Bridge; train to Deptford; bus 188 to stop A, Deptford High Street | Hours Daily noon–11.30pm, food served Mon–Sat noon–3.30pm & 6–9pm, Sun 12.30–3.30pm | Tip While the Dog and Bell has been defying gentrification, the latter has not been all bad, bringing some good independent breweries. One of these can be found under the arcades of Deptford Station: check out Villages Brewery (21-22 Resolution Way).

21 East Greenwich Pleasaunce

Sailors came to rest, children come to play

When the Royal Park is a hive of activity, Greenwich residents head to the East Greenwich Pleasaunce. It's their secret green-space, hidden behind houses and only a mile away from its larger cousin. This tree-lined garden provides peace and relaxation, and is very popular with families. Its name is derived from an old-French word meaning pleasure-garden. It even has a little *'je ne sais quoi'* of Gallic airiness with its attractive eco-friendly café, Pistachios in the Park, a charming *estaminet*, with tables and chairs spilling out from the terrace onto the grass. In truth, however, this park has no French connection. Historians have suggested that it was named after Greenwich Palace, known as a Pleasaunce. This little park was originally an orchard. In 1857, the Admiralty bought it to expand their burial grounds. In 1875, around 3,000 bodies were re-buried here to make way for the extension of the railway. Sailors who fought at the Battle of Trafalgar, Crimea and during two World Wars were laid to rest according to naval etiquette, with seamen in the west plot, and officers in the east.

In 1926, it was turned over to the Council. Since then, the dead and the living have shared the space in perfect harmony. The Pleasaunce is also child-friendly, with a playground and dedicated play centre. The trees nearby are a popular spot for an impromptu ball game. A dedicated Friends Group never misses an occasion to organise all sorts of events: gigs, fetes, cinema viewings, and Bopping Bunnies' shows, to name but a few. October sees the Battle of Trafalgar celebrations, and with January comes the 'Wassail': a traditional time to 'drink to the fruits' in the two new orchards, in the company of the 'Holly Man'. When there is nothing official on the calendar, locals make it up, put fancy dresses on the children, and the party begins.

Address 10 Chevening Road, London, SE10 0LB; the main entrance is on Chevening Road, and there's a smaller gate half-way up Halstow Road | Getting there Bus 108, 177, 188, 286 or 422 to Marlton Street or Kemsing Road; train to Westcombe Park (Southeastern & Thameslink); tube to North Greenwich (Jubilee Line), then bus 188 or 422 | Hours Summer, daily 9am–6pm; winter, daily 9am–5pm | Tip Vice Admiral Hardy is the Greenwich resident best known for being Nelson's friend, and the man to hear Nelson's last words. His body was not interred in 1875, but remained in the officers' vault in Greenwich Hospital Cemetery, in the grounds of Devonport House adjacent to the Maritime Museum (see ch. 37).

22 The Ecology Park
Escape to the Wild Side

From factory to wildlife haven, this former steelworks site, situated in the Millennium Village, has certainly changed a lot. With just over four acres, in an otherwise densely built environment, the Ecology Park offers a lot for its size: two freshwater lakes surrounded by marshland, a small Alder woodland, and a walk-in wildflower meadow.

Leave the concert-goers at the doors of the O2 Arena and meet the local residents, none of which has been artificially introduced. Newts, toads, frogs, colourful dragonflies, bats, even a rare moth – they've all found their way back to this natural habitat. Being situated within sight of Canary Wharf, the only high fliers you'll spot in the park are Common Snipe, Water Rail, Grebes, Gulls and a few other species. Bird-watching is done from the comfort of specially designed viewing huts. The two shelters contain folders with information and a board to keep a record of visitors – the avian kind, that is.

The Ecology Park, managed by the Trust for Urban Ecology, was a partnership project as part of the Peninsula redevelopment. Since its launch in 2002, the park has become a popular community feature, cherished by local children. The park is easily accessible with a buggy or wheelchair thanks to the wooden boardwalks. Volunteers have set up quiz trails for visitors to follow. The information also ensures that nobody misses an important sight. This is an excellent activity to learn a little about the history of Greenwich Peninsula, a lot about the native fauna and flora, and how a once natural wetland buzzing with life became so polluted by several decades of environmentally harmful industrialisation that most species were displaced. Events for children such as pond-dipping and bug-hunting often take place. Three times a year there's also a frog day. The wildflower meadow is a great place for a friends and family picnic, but there's no on-site café, so plan your escape to the wild accordingly.

Address Thames Path, John Harrison Way, London, SE10 0QZ, www.thelandtrust.org.uk | **Getting there** Tube to North Greenwich (Jubilee Line); bus 108, 129, 161, 472 or 486 to Millennium Village; boat to North Greenwich Pier from east and west London; Emirates Air Line Cable Car across the Thames from Royal Victoria Dock, close to Royal Victoria DLR station | **Hours** See website | **Tip** There's a lot of green space in Greenwich, so to help you find your way around all these parks and open spaces, use the Urban Good *National Park City Greenwich Map* – www.urbangood.org.

23   Eltham Palace

Art Deco elegance meets medieval sensation

Eltham Palace is renowned for its spectacular 1930s interiors, created for the Courtaulds. This unlikely juxtaposition of medieval and modern in many ways mirrors Stephen and Virginia Courtauld's marriage: he, one of two heirs to a textile fortune, thoughtful and serious; she, a flamboyant and eccentric divorcée who claimed to be a descendant of Vlad the Impaler. They met while holidaying in the romantic Italian Lakes, where they married in 1923.

In the 1930s, they acquired the lease to Eltham Palace. By then, this royal abode, with its illustrious past, was mostly dilapidated. The Courtaulds obtained permission from the Crown estate to build a new house in the grounds, on condition that they restored the Great Hall. The manor is recorded in the 1086 Domesday survey. It was gifted to Edward II in 1305, and Henry VIII enjoyed the palace for tournaments and parties. The refurbished medieval hall is a splendour, with its great hammer-beam roof – the third-largest of its kind in England after Westminster Hall and Christ Church in Oxford. The stained glass windows commemorate the kings and queens of its past, and there's also a minstrel's gallery.

The house is a luxurious Art Deco space, with all mod-cons and cutting-edge communications technology. The family commissioned Siemens to install a sophisticated private internal telephone exchange throughout the house. There's under-floor heating, synchronised wall clocks and loudspeakers all over the house for music. Virginia's bathroom, designed by Malacrida, is top-to-toe in onyx, slate and gold mosaic. Stephen's reminders are sober, such as *The Sentry* – a beautiful bronze by Jagger, the heir's comrade-in-arms during World War I. This is not the only reminder of the war, as there's also an underground reinforced war room. And it wouldn't have been their home without a heated jungle room for Virginia's lemur, Mah-Jongg.

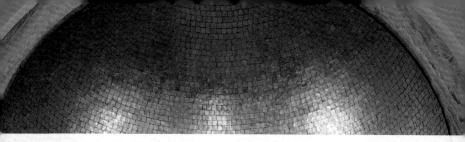

Address Court Yard, London, SE9 5QE, English Heritage, +44 (0)370 333 1181, www.english-heritage.org.uk/visit/places/eltham-palace-and-gardens | Getting there Train to Mottingham; tube to North Greenwich (Jubilee Line); bus 132 to Eltham Church Well Hall Road | Hours See website for current information on visiting and tours | Tip Burton the Tailor's former store in the centre of Greenwich, at the corner of Nelson Road and Greenwich Church Street, opened in an amazing Art Deco building in 1932. Now a Bill's restaurant, the most striking features on the sublime façade are several elephant heads – look up and enjoy.

24 Emirates Air Line

Get a bird's-eye view of London

The Emirates Air Line Cable Car covers the distance between the Greenwich Peninsula by the O2 Arena and the Royal Docks on the north side of the Thames. The idea came about as part of the 2012 Olympics. As a commuters' route, it's not hugely popular, but it's a hit with tourists and delegates attending trade fairs at the ExCel Centre. This urban cable car is the first in the capital, and so far the only one, so expect rides to be popular at weekends and during school holidays. The cabins are spacious. The red seats are upholstered in the famous style of the Tube moquette. A video with audio commentaries is the newest addition for the benefit of passengers. The staff at both ends are diligent and might even offer your party a cabin of its own, if available. When London transport is frantic at best of time, here there's no rush, and no long queues – everything is geared towards enjoyment.

Once in the air, the cabins cruise 90 metres above ground – don't forget to give a little wave to the passengers travelling in the opposite direction. The pods feel safe even on windy days, taking an average of five minutes to make the journey – 13 at night. On a clear day, the experience offers breathtaking aerial views. Looking at the O2 Arena from this vantage point certainly beats the opening credits of *EastEnders!*

The Thames Barrier shines like a star whilst the quiet video guide provides food for thought. Once near City Airport, with a bit of luck, you'll get to see a plane landing: only special aircraft and crew certified to fly 5.5-degree approaches – twice the normal angle – can operate at London City Airport. Even though the capital skyline is spectacular, it's almost beaten by the sight of East End regeneration taking place on the north side of the river. Without any doubt, these London districts are moving away from their industrial past. This is a unique way to get a 360 degree bird's-eye view of this gigantic urban transformation.

Address Unit 1, 2, 3 & 4 Emirates Cable Car Terminal, Edmund Halley Way, London, SE10 0FR, +44 (0)343 222 1234, www.tfl.gov.uk/modes/emirates-air-line | Getting there By boat from central London piers to The O2; bus 188; tube to North Greenwich (Jubilee Line); on foot from Greenwich centre via the river path | Hours Mon–Thu 7–9pm, Fri 7–11pm, Sat 8–11pm, Sun & bank holidays 9–9pm; tickets for a single journey cost £3.50 per adult with Oyster card and travel card holders, £4.50 for non-card holders | Tip There's just one lighthouse in London – at the artists' hub of Trinity Buoy Wharf – and it holds something pretty special: a 1,000-year-long, non-repeating musical composition performed by computers using Tibetan singing bowls. So far, Jem Finer's *Longplayer* has been on for nearly 20 years. Trinity Buoy Wharf also has a sculpture park and a tiny museum.

25 Enderby Wharf

Where the internet had its beginnings

Enderby Wharf is an important historical site on the Greenwich Peninsula. This wharf is associated with the 'Atlantic Cables' used for telegraph communications between Europe and the rest of the world. This technology revolutionised communications, transformed the City of London, and set it on its way to being one of the world's most important financial centres.

The Enderbys were oil and chemical merchants who married into the Buxton whaling family. Their fleet played an important role in recording Antarctica. One of their ships was immortalised in Melville's novel *Moby Dick*. In 1846, Charles Enderby had a riverside home built on the wharf. The white house, with its 'Octagon Room', is now a pub. By the mid-19th century the area was still covered by marshes and prone to flooding. It's ironic, then, that a fire ravaged the Enderby's factory, and marked the start of a slow decline for the family's fortunes. Subsequently, the jetty and causeway fell into disuse, until the land was bought by Glass, Elliot & Co to manufacture submarine cables. It's here that, in 1857, the first attempt was made to lay a telegraph cable across the Atlantic.

Nowadays, as the wharf is a large residential development, a few structures of that period remain. Opposite the white house, look for steps and a causeway leading down to the river. These were used to row crew out to the cable ships. They were restored beautifully and carved by local sculptor, Richard Lawrence. However, the most striking structures are the tall grey steel tower and the wheel engine cable. Both tell the story of a 125-year period when Greenwich and Woolwich Siemens led the world in submarine cable manufacture. One of the two Enderby jetties has been planted with 'squidgy bits' that act as a landing platform for wetland birds such as cormorants, geese, and wagtails – an ecological addition to an industrial past.

Address Enderby Wharf, Olympian Way, London, SE10 0TA | Getting there Bus 108, 129, 177, 180, 188, 286 or 386 to Tyler Street, then take Christchurch and Pelton Road towards the river, where you can join the river path; the river has a cycle lane; no cars allowed on the riverside path | Hours Enderby Wharf is a public path, open 24/7 throughout the year | Tip The various shaped columns next to the white house are parts of a sculpture called *Lay Lines*, which replicates the forms of various important cables. A QR code on the wall leads to digital information.

26 The Fan Museum
A fan-tastic place to visit

You'll find the Fan Museum housed in two adjacent Grade II-listed Georgian buildings in Greenwich historic centre. Founded in 1991 by Helene Alexander MBE and her husband Dicky, this fascinating collection is entirely devoted to the history of fans, fan leaves and their making. With more than 6,000 fans from around the world, this museum is unique. The oldest fan in the collection dates from the 10th century. Some of the museum's most stunning pieces are jewelled, delicately embedded with precious stones or piqués and cloutés with mother of pearl; others are playful, designed for flirting and peek-a-boo. Each fan is a delight to look at and this remarkable museum is well worth a visit. Around 2,000 pieces are from the owners' collection, while others have been acquired, gifted, or donated by bequest.

The most prestigious are fans decorated by famous masters, an exotic landscape by Gauguin, a theatre scene painted by Sickert. The finest were used by royalty and the aristocracy. On display is a very rare Elizabethan fan made of embroidered silk and metallic threads, that dates from around 1550 – a time when folding fans were not yet the norm in Europe, only appearing around 1580. The exhibits change three times a year, with guest exhibits showcasing highlights and other collections. In 2017, the Fan Museum launched a pioneering project to put fan-making on the map. Based on a concept by Europe's foremost contemporary fan-maker, Codex Urbanus, 29 street artists created a series of innovative fans, which were subsequently displayed in a landmark exhibition.

If you fancy trying fan-making yourself, the museum is increasing its number of workshops. If that wasn't enough, there's an exceptional library and a beautiful muraled orangery where afternoon tea is served to groups. This lovely tea room faces a fan-shaped Japanese garden. Definitely a must-see for visitors and locals alike.

Address The Fan Museum, 12 Crooms Hill, London, SE10 8ER, +44 (0)20 8305 1441, www.thefanmuseum.org.uk | **Getting there** DLR or train to Cutty Sark or Greenwich | **Hours** Tue–Sat 11am–5pm, Sun, Mon & bank holidays noon–5pm; adults £5, concessions and children 7–16 £3, children under 7 go free; 50% discount for National Trust members | **Tip** Crooms Hill is an ancient road, and may be the oldest known road in London. Its name comes from 'crom', meaning crooked in Celtic. Follow it to the top to admire its imposing houses, some of which are open to the public once a year on National Open Day.

27___Gallions Reach Park

Explore south-east London's very own pyramids!

We like to think of these as south-east London's pyramids: a series of roughly pyramidal structures, one larger than the others, next to a housing estate! Gallions Hill is one of south-east London's least-known landmarks. It's a little bit off the beaten track, but so was Giza once upon a time, and while the building of these majestic mounds can't compare with the pyramids, it was nonetheless a monumental task. Formerly part of the Royal Arsenal, they were made out of the rubble left over from the construction of the local housing here, in order to create a viewpoint that is one of the best for miles around.

It's a job well done, and a focal point in what is perhaps one of the most maligned neighbourhoods in Greenwich borough: Thamesmead, a mainly 1970s residential area created from much of the original Royal Arsenal's land. It was cutting-edge at the time, but also the epitome of an alienating urban environment – hence its use in key parts of Stanley Kubrick's dystopian film *A Clockwork Orange*, as well as numerous music videos over the years. Part of the newer development of West Thamesmead, Gallions Reach represents the area's renaissance as a genuinely pleasant and appealing place to live, a much more accessible neighbourhood with far better facilities, in stark contrast to its previous image.

You can follow the snail's shell path up the main tor of the park for impressive 360-degree views over the river. If the picnic spot at the top isn't that impressive – just a few benches and a tarmacked area – the views certainly compensate, taking in Shooters Hill, Kent, Essex, Canary Wharf and The City, and of course the river itself at Gallions Reach. Once you've tired of the views, follow the gentle path down to the bottom and then wind through the other smaller tors and pyramids down to the riverfront and the Thames Path, where you can turn left for Gallions Park playground and lake.

Address 22 Defence Close, London, SE28 0NU | Getting there Bus 380 to West Thamesmead; train to Plumstead, then a 20-minute walk | Hours Always open | Tip Thamesmead is now one of Greenwich's major wildlife havens, its marshy landscape fragmented by several lakes. Closest to Gallions Reach, the former munitions store of Tump 53 has also been revived as a small, family-friendly nature reserve.

28 General Wolfe Statue

Could this be London's best view?

Although less than a century old, the statue of General Wolfe, set on a plinth at the end of Greenwich Park's tree-lined central avenue, and perfectly aligned with the Queen's House and Royal Naval College below and Blackheath's Church of All Saints in the opposite direction, is about as iconic a Greenwich sight as you'll find. Not only that – the view it enjoys is surely one of London's best: the perfect symmetry of Greenwich spreads beyond the green of the park to the backdrop of the glass-fronted towers of Docklands on the far side of the river, with the dome of the O2 to the right, and far-off towers of the City, including The Shard, to the left.

The statue itself is a general gathering and lounging point for tourists enjoying the view and decompressing after visiting the observatory – as well as a monument to one of Britain's greatest military heroes, General James Wolfe, and his victory against the French at Quebec in 1759. The battle succeeded in securing Canada for the British, but saw Wolfe lose his life, turning him into a military martyr whose fame was only exceeded by Nelson half a century later.

Wolfe had fought at Culloden and other landmark battles, and was a hero in the truest sense. A humble and driven commander who never married, he carried a musket like his men, and was renowned for being tough and single-minded. Wolfe died on the battlefield at the age of 32 but lived much of his life in Greenwich, where he lay in state before being buried next to his father in the church of St Alfege. A plaque remembers him in the church, and there's another, more lavish monument showing his death in Westminster Abbey, while a number of local roads and even a primary school are named after him. Oddly enough, there's also a road named after the Marquis of Montcalm, whom Wolfe defeated at Quebec, and whose descendant unveiled the statue in 1930.

Address Greenwich Park, London, SE10 8QY | **Getting there** DLR to Cutty Sark; train to Greenwich or Maze Hill; bus 129, 177, 180, 188, 199, 286 or 386 to Greenwich town centre | **Hours** Always open | **Tip** After seeing the statue wander across to see the blue plaque on the park-facing wall of McCartney House at the top of Crooms Hill where Wolfe lived as a child – just walk out of the gate to get to the front of the house, which is now a series of privately owned flats.

29 Greenwich Foot Tunnel
Take a walk beneath the Thames

Controversies around Thames crossings, or the lack thereof, are not new. In the early 1900s, crossing by ferry was hazardous, especially in the dark. When the air pollution was dense, and the infamous London fog so thick, visibility was so poor that reaching the other bank could never be guaranteed! This was a real problem during the Industrial Revolution and for the workers who lived south of the river: they needed a reliable, all-weather means of commuting to the Isle of Dogs' shipyards and docks. The problem started to disrupt the economy and the growth of the metropolis. As a result, an act of parliament was passed, and not one but two tunnels under the river were built: one in Greenwich, one in Woolwich.

With its white ceramic tiles and York stone flags, the Greenwich tunnel almost looks plain, but it's an amazing Edwardian engineering feat that took only three years to complete. The underwater crossing is 370 metres long and 15 metres deep on very complex terrain. To put this in perspective, in 2009, when the tunnel needed restoration to bring it into the 21st century, the work lasted five years. From the day it opened in 1902, it proved very popular, and by 1905 over 9,000 people were using it weekly. The Blitz was a disaster for the dock, and the tunnel was damaged on the first day. This is why the ceramic tiles stop three-quarters of the way, and the northern side is covered with an internal steel sleeve.

One of the 2009 restoration tasks was the replacement of the entrance Grade II-listed glass dome, which, after 120 years, had become extremely dirty. To keep the familiar look, an engineered dirty layer was created with a faint smoky tint. This is a very atmospheric place at any time of day, but even more so at night: if you hear disembodied voices or footsteps, it's probably because the three resident ghosts have decided to keep you company!

Address Under the Thames between Greenwich and Island Garden on the Isle of Dogs/ Millwall | Getting there Train to Greenwich; boat, MBNA Thames Clippers depart from all major London piers every 20 minutes; bus 53, 54, 129, 177, 180, 188, 199, 202, 286, 380, 386 or N1 to Cutty Sark | Hours Open 24 hours; the tunnel is accessible by spiral staircase, or lift at each end | Tip It's well worth crossing the river to take a look at Greenwich from the northern bank: the view, often depicted by artists such as Canaletto, is spectacular.

30__Greenwich Market

Greenwich's beating heart

To Londoners, at least, Greenwich is known for its market. Indeed, once upon a time markets filled every available open space in the town centre at weekends, selling everything from crafts and food to bric-a-brac, antiques and old furniture. The area now occupied by the Greenwich University library, between the railway line and Nevada Street, was in particular a source of all kinds of junk, and attracted treasure-hunters from all over London. The real market, though, has always been the rectangle at the centre of the town's one-way system. This was hollowed out of the winding medieval streets in the 19th century by Joseph Kay, to create the covered market square you see today.

You can get a sense of the original street plan on narrow Turnpin Lane, which winds its way into the market from opposite St Alfege Church (see ch. 87). In a way it seems a shame to have lost what must have been a unique, bustling urban environment. But Kay's market plan is undeniably fit for purpose, and lends a functional grandeur to proceedings, with corniced, clearly marked entrance arches, including a pillared entrance next to the Admiral Hardy pub, inscribed with the grave slogan: *A false balance is an abomination to the Lord but a just weight is his delight*. It's a motto that somehow suited the market at the time, which dealt mainly in fruit and veg and goods that people actually needed. Alas, it's less appropriate for the crafty clothes and candles, lamps and pictures that are generally on sale here these days. It remains a vibrant part of central Greenwich, however, crammed with people at weekends. Consequently, its owners Greenwich Hospital Estates have spent handsomely on its upkeep in recent years, replacing the roof and building a covered food court next door to house the multiple street food cuisines on offer, from oysters and fish and chips to jerk chicken and churros. Load up your plate and stroll down to the riverside for a perfect alfresco lunch by the water.

Address London, SE10 9HZ | Getting there Train to Greenwich; DLR to Cutty Sark; bus 129, 177, 180, 188, 199, 286 or 386 to Greenwich town centre | Hours Daily 10am–5.30pm | Tip Greenwich retains a few elements of its bric-a-brac roots in a couple of spots that spring up at weekends, most notably a small triangle of land just past the NatWest Bank, where you can buy everything from ancient football programmes to old furniture, and a slightly larger affair next to the cinema, whose stalls sell old porcelain, jewellery, rare vinyl, and lots of other potentially serendipitous finds.

31 Greenwich Park Bandstand
Musical feature that strikes a chord with many

In their heyday, over 1,200 bandstands graced public parks, piers, lidos or other leisure spaces in the United Kingdom. Their primary aim was to drag punters away from pubs by providing free entertainment in the open air, in doing so improving health and cultural well-being. The concept was immediately popular with people up and down Britain.

During World War II many bandstands were broken up out of necessity, their structures being melted down to provide metal for the Military. As a result, only just over 350 bandstands of the original number were left standing. One of those that survived is located in Greenwich Park. It's in the middle of the appropriately named Band Field, bordered by majestic Sweet Chestnut and Hawthorn trees. This pagoda-style bandstand is a fine example of ironwork, and a beautiful Grade II-listed building. The green and red hexagonal structure stands on a white base, decorated with jet black iron railings. The Coalbrook-dale Company, famous for its decorative ironwork, produced the roof frame, while Dean & Co assembled it and installed the iron columns.

On 4 June, 1891, the Greenwich bandstand was opened with a performance by the Northumberland Fusiliers Band from nearby Woolwich. It marked the start of a series of Thursday evening performances during that summer. The local newspaper of the time reported that, despite the rain, 5,000 people attended the opening concert and enjoyed a well-chosen selection of popular melodies. From the 1950s onward, it was used for occasional music events only.

In 2013, The Friends of Greenwich Park revived the Victorian stage's fortune, and free Sunday afternoon concerts are once again regularly performed during the summer. These range from jazz orchestras and military bands, to swing ensembles and rock and roll groups. The nation's taste in music may have changed, but the benefits of enjoying music outdoors remain.

Address Greenwich Park, London, SE10 8QY | Getting there Train to Greenwich; DLR to Cutty Sark; bus 129, 177, 180, 188, 199, 286 or 386 to Greenwich town centre | Hours See website for current information on visiting | Tip In 1891, the year the bandstand opened, a Victorian granite drinking fountain was installed in the park by Blackheath Gate; in 2019, five new water fountains were erected in the Royal Borough in an effort to reduce the waste from plastic bottles.

32 — Greenwich Park Wildlife

Birds, bats, deer… and parakeets!

Greenwich Park is worth a visit at any time of year, but what most people don't realise is that it's a hotbed of nature and wildlife – a Grade I-listed landscape and Site of Metropolitan Importance for Nature Conservation. Indeed, it always has been, since it served as the deer park and hunting ground of Henry VIII in the 16th century.

The deer remain, and the Greenwich herds occupy a large chunk of the park's south-eastern corner. Originally used to roaming throughout the park, they were enclosed in the so-called 'Wilderness' area during the 1920s. There are two herds of red and fallow deer, many of which are descended from the original deer of Henry VIII. They're routinely visible from a viewing point, accessible from the park's flower gardens by way of a couple of converging woodland paths. The park's Wildlife Centre, located in the deer park itself, also offers an opportunity for a closer look, and there are plans to install a learning centre and café with an added woodland trail that will make it much easier to see the deer.

The park also has plenty of other critters, such as tiny pipistrelle bats, which come out at dusk to feed on the park's plentiful insect population, 14 species of butterfly, and no less than 92 different kinds of spider! There are more species of birds than you might expect to find in a city park, too, including woodpeckers, warblers and even owls. Most notorious of all, however, are the noisy parakeets, whose population has spread from south-west London over the last decade or so. These are the 'Marmite' of birds: people either love the parakeets or hate them – but what they can't do is ignore them, as they squawk and squabble among the trees above, piercing the peace of even a solitary stroll. Catch them – along with the park's other feathered friends – on Sunday morning bird walks at 8.30am each week, organised by the Friends of Greenwich Park.

Address The Wilderness Deer Park, Greenwich Park, London, SE10 8QY | Getting there Bus 53 stops right outside; train to Blackheath, then a short walk across the Heath | Hours See website for current information on visiting | Tip There are guided walks for members of the 'Friends of Greenwich Park' on selected days – see www.friendsofgreenwichpark.org.uk for details, and watch out also for the new Vanbrugh Café due to open soon nearby.

33 Greenwich Theatre

An off-West End theatre with a proud tradition

Situated at the bottom of Crooms Hill near the park, Greenwich is proud of its theatre – a former music hall that has long been a local landmark and to some extent continues a dramatic tradition that started with the regular performances of the Richardson travelling theatre here in the 19th century.

The theatre was renovated in the middle of the last century, and under its artistic director, Ewan Hooper, established a low-key reputation in the 1960s for distinguished and sometimes cutting-edge productions. The venue attracted big names of the day, such as Susannah York, Vivien Merchant and local thespian Glenda Jackson, playing roles in weighty, well-chosen works like *The Three Sisters*, *The Vortex* and *Miss Julie*, not to mention featuring local stalwart and cult comedian Max Wall in cult productions like Samuel Beckett's *Krapp's Last Tape*. In those days, Wall could often be found propping up the theatre bar, which in those days was a popular watering-hole for actorly types and bohemian folk. In the 1980s the theatre premiered John Mortimer's *Voyage around My Father* and staged Rupert Everett's *Another Country*, but sadly the 1990s saw a period of decline: the theatre's subsidy was withdrawn, and it was temporarily closed during the latter part of the decade.

However, since re-opening at the end of 1999 it has flowered again, focusing more on short-run seasonal productions, musicals and family entertainment than the chancy contemporary fare for which it used to be known. Most famously the theatre has established a considerable reputation for superlative Christmas pantomimes under the direction of Andrew Pollard. These are eagerly awaited each year, and sell out almost immediately. Either way, it's a terrific place to see a play or show, intimate without being poky, and with a thrust (rather than proscenium) stage, which creates a really intimate feel.

Address National Maritime Museum, Romney Road, London, SE10 9NF | **Getting there** Train to Greenwich or Maze Hill; DLR to Cutty Sark; bus 129, 177, 180, 188, 199, 286 or 386 to Greenwich town centre | **Hours** Open for performances | **Tip** A blue plaque records the fact that Poet Laureate Cecil Day-Lewis lived in the elegant Georgian house at 6 Crooms Hill opposite the theatre: appropriate, given that one of the greatest British actors of his generation – his son Daniel – grew up there.

34 Greenwich Yacht Club
Three Men in a Boat, it is not!

The upper reaches of the Thames tend to be slow, meandering and bucolic – the peaceful domain of lovers, rowers, boating enthusiasts and drinkers sipping ale in sunny riverside pubs. But the lower reaches of the Thames are a different matter: grittier and more historic, with industry and commerce and their associated infrastructure intensifying the further east you travel. The handsome waterfront of central Greenwich provides some light relief, but the urban feel intensifies as you round the second half of the curve around the Isle of Dogs. *Three Men in a Boat*, this is not... That doesn't mean that getting out on the river isn't desirable, however. Here, the river is wider than further upstream, making it all the more appealing for weekend sailors, for whom Greenwich Yacht Club has provided a boatyard, moorings and tuition for over a century.

Originally founded by a group of Thames watermen and other river workers in 1908, the yacht club in Greenwich has always been a more down-to-earth affair than most, which have a certain reputation for being a little snobbish. Perhaps not coincidentally, this club is also one of the largest and most popular on the Thames, with over 400 members. There's also a new clubhouse, which opened just after the Millennium with funding from English Partnerships – an upgrade from the retired Thames sailing barge the club previously used, *Iverna*, located on the beach nearby.

The building itself is worthy of note: a flat-roofed steel and glass structure on stilts above the river, reached by a causeway that leads from the boatyard. It's home to a bar and restaurant that's well worth a visit if you get the chance – not just for a drink in one of the river's most unusual buildings, but also for a look at some of the old photos of the club that line the walls. Look out, too, for the club's open days for novice sailors and RYA events.

Address 1 Peartree Way, London, SE10 0BW, +44 (0)20 8396 0321, www.greenwichyachtclub.co.uk | Getting there Tube to Greenwich (Jubilee Line); bus 129, 132, 161, 335, 472 or 486 to Millennium Village Oval Square, then walk across Ecology Park | Hours Clubhouse open Tuesday evenings and all day at weekends | Tip Boat-lovers might also want to check out the Curlew Rowing Club, founded in 1866, which has a beautifully situated riverside HQ on Crane Street, next door to the Trafalgar Tavern (see ch. 99).

35   Heap's Sausages and Café
Heap Heap Hooray for award-winning sausages

Soon after butcher Bill O'Hagan left his Greenwich premises to open a shop at the seaside, locals displayed withdrawal symptoms. People were exchanging the names of potential suppliers of bangers, but nothing seemed satisfactory. Since the 1980s, they had bought their supplies in one of Britain's top sausage shops. In 2012, when it became known that Martin Heap had chosen Greenwich for his next venture and was to open shop in a small street near the park entrance, the news spread like wildfire.

The owner's reputation had preceded his arrival. It was common knowledge that Martin Heap was London's leading sausage-maker since 1991, with his brand Simply Sausages, and locals were hoping for similar quality. Nobody was disappointed when Heap and his business partner Enzo Carbonara started making sausages at the back of the premises, in an open-plan workshop. Their best-seller is the award-winning Heap's N1 sausage, in natural skin. The exact recipe of this uniquely flavoured creation is a closely-guarded secret, but eggs, nutmeg, coriander and mace all feature in the mix, along with a special selection of other spices. The menu is seasonal: expect Bramley apples and chestnut flavours in the autumn, spring onions and chilli when the weather gets brighter, and of course turkey and Christmas spices in December.

It's not only about take-away sausages, though. Heap's is a convenient place to buy a quick bite, the 'Lethal Lucifer' 10-inch hot-dog with honey fried onions on a brioche is a customer favourite. The shop also offers artisan bread, with the big Heap's bap most popular. The shop shelves are filled with wine, locally brewed beers, speciality grocery items and ham. Indoor and outdoor seating offers an opportunity for groups to meet, with people tucking into a full-English or savouring a sausage roll from the all-day menu a familiar scene.

Address 8 Nevada Street, London, SE10 9JL, +44 (0)20 8293 9199, www.heapssausages.com |
Getting there Train or DLR to Greenwich, then a five-minute walk towards Greenwich Park
main entrance; Heap's is opposite Greenwich Theatre | Hours Mon–Fri 7.30am–4pm,
Sat & Sun 9am–4pm | Tip If you love traditional English food, get a table at Goddards,
for pie, liquor and mash – a family business since 1890, serving traditional pie & mash for
around £5.00 (www.goddardsatgreenwich.co.uk).

36 Henry Moore's Knife Edge

Curious incident of the statue in the night-time

When one morning in 2007, Greenwich residents woke to find an empty space where once stood a 3.5-metre bronze sculpture weighing over a tonne by Henry Moore. The initial assumption was theft, but this was dismissed on account of the bronze's monumental scale. But then the question remained: what had happened to *Large Standing Figure: Knife Edge*? The sculpture is part of a series of 13 similar bronzes started in 1961. The artist, whose sculptures can be found in public places all over the world, personally selected the exact location for his giant bronze sculpture, and chose the specific piece to be installed in Greenwich. One of only two original casts, the sculpture was installed on its plinth in 1979. Moore's inspiration for this bronze was a small fragment of a bird's breastbone. In an essay, the sculptor talks about his early fascination for bones, and how he '...Found them on sea-shores and saved them out of the stew pot ... Some bones, such as the breast bones of birds, have the lightweight fineness of a knife-blade.'

With much speculation regarding the disappearance, it transpired that The Henry Moore Foundation was responsible for the statue's removal: it was taken on an international tour, then placed in storage. The official justification for the statue's sudden disappearance was that the Foundation was increasingly worried about the prospect of vandalism by graffiti. This explanation didn't satisfy the local press, however, and it was alleged that the foundation had demanded a large rise in indemnity from the Royal Parks. By mid-2011, just as the park's supporters had given up hope of a reappearance of *Large Standing Figure: Knife Edge*, the sculpture was returned to its original location, just in time for the 2012 Olympic games, whereupon it received a hero's welcome. For the foreseeable future, the work will remain in Greenwich.

Address 1 Park Walk, London, SE10 8HT | Getting there Access the park via the main entrance, St Mary's Gate, walk along The Avenue, take the fifth path on the right; be prepared to walk uphill | Hours Daily 6am–6pm (hours vary by season) | Tip Moore's is not the only large sculpture to do a disappearing act: next to the Trafalgar Tavern, a life-sized bronze of Lord Nelson stands facing the river, and this piece also disappeared temporarily, in even more mysterious circumstances…

37 The Hospital Mausoleum

Sealed with a kiss? Hardy's last resting place

Greenwich has many reminders of Nelson, but perhaps one of the most surprising is the old graveyard of the former Greenwich Hospital in front of Devonport House, next to the Maritime Museum. This is where the bodies of dead seamen were brought from what used to be the Dreadnought Naval Hospital across the road. Some 24,000 men were buried here at one time; now it's given over to a handful of scattered tombs and gravestones, mixed in with a few bee-hives and the brick-built Greenwich Hospital Mausoleum – the last resting-place of one Thomas Masterman Hardy. It was Hardy who served for many years with Nelson, and was memorably invited to kiss the admiral on his death bed at the Battle of Trafalgar.

Hardy was the Governor of Greenwich Hospital for five years and passed away in 1839 at the age of 70. His coffin lies along with many others in a lower ground floor vault, and contains a miniature of the revered admiral that Nelson gave to Hardy before his death. Sadly, the mausoleum is normally railed off, so visitors have to content themselves with a view of the outside and a walk in the gardens. Here, a nearby monument remembers Tom Allen, Nelson's faithful manservant who, despite not being a seaman, was an occupant of the hospital and died here in 1838. Allen was with the admiral for almost the whole of his career, and was among other things an important go-between during Nelson's affair with Lady Hamilton. It's said Allen never forgave himself for not being with the admiral when he fell at Trafalgar, but Hardy was magnanimous enough to make sure he got this suitably grand memorial.

Hardy himself is more modestly remembered, with a diminutive oak tree planted in front of the mausoleum in 2014, on the 180th anniversary of his appointment as the hospital's governor. Check it out before heading off to see his bust in the Royal Naval College chapel.

Address Romney Road, London, SE10 9NF | Getting there Train to Greenwich or Maze Hill; DLR to Cutty Sark; bus 129, 177, 180, 188, 199, 286 or 386 to Greenwich town centre | Hours Open house days only | Tip There are other naval burial places dotted around Greenwich, most famously East Greenwich Pleasaunce (see ch. 21) and also a lesser-known, one-storey arched mausoleum on Maze Hill, which is believed to have been designed by the architect of St Alfege's, Nicholas Hawksmoor. Unfortunately you can't visit – it's in the grounds of a private house, and is now used as a garden shed!

38 Ignatius Sancho Plaque

The first black Briton to own property and vote

Ignatius Sancho achieved a few firsts in his lifetime. Said to have been born aboard a slave ship bound for the West Indies in 1729, Sancho led an extraordinary life, and was the first person of African descent to be given an obituary in the British press.

Soon after his birth, his mother died and his father committed suicide to avoid a life of slavery. Aged two, Sancho was brought to England by his master, and given as a slave-child to three maiden sisters who lived in Greenwich. In the early 18th century, black domestics were like fashion accessories, and the sisters were not very kind to him. But since Ignatius was a personable child, he befriended a neighbour, the Duke of Montagu. Montagu took Sancho under his wing, gave him the free run of his library, paid for his education, and eventually employed him as his personal butler. It was as a direct result of Montagu's encouragement and influence that Ignatius Sancho became a literary figure and composer.

Aged 30, he married Anne Osbourne, a woman of African descent, and the couple had seven children. By then, Sancho was a prolific writer of poetry and political letters, his lobbying instrumental in the fight against slavery. In the mid-1760s, Gainsborough painted Sancho's portrait. Around that time he became ill with gout and was unable to work as a butler any longer. As a result, the Montagu family bought him a shop in Westminster selling sweets, tea and tobacco. Although a sweet shop may not have been the best choice for a person with ill-health. Thanks to Sancho's gregariousness the shop soon attracted political celebrities, and the elite of London arts society. Furthermore, as a shop owner, Sancho was able to cast his vote in a British parliamentary election, and in doing so, blazed a trail for black Africans in Britain. Ignatius Sancho died in December 1780, leaving behind an important body of writing and music.

Address Chesterfield Gate, Greenwich Park, London, SE10 8QY | **Getting there** Bus 53 or 386 to Chesterfield Gate/Greenwich Park; 25-minute walk (mostly uphill) from Greenwich town centre and head towards the top of the park to the Rose Garden | **Hours** Daily 6am–6pm (hours vary by season) | **Tip** To understand the transatlantic slave trade, head to the Atlantic gallery on the first floor of National Maritime Museum.

39___Italo Svevo's House

Literary Italy comes to the heart of Charlton

Charlton is full of surprises, and one of the nicest and most unexpected is the blue plaque on the wall of 67 Charlton Church Lane, which remembers the 20th-century Italian writer Italo Svevo – otherwise known as 'Ettore Schmitz'. Schmitz lived here from 1903 to 1913, and briefly again after World War I, when working for an Italian firm owned by his father-in-law. They established a factory in nearby Anchor & Hope Lane, partly to supply anti-corrosive paint for the ships of the Royal Navy, and Svevo was lucky enough to be sent over to south-east London to manage operations.

A native of Trieste, now in north-east Italy but then one of the major ports of the Austro-Hungarian Empire, Svevo was a talented writer and a protégé of his English teacher, James Joyce, who famously lived in the city for a while. Joyce promoted Svevo's best-known work, *Confessions of Zeno*, which was published when the author was in his 60s. It's an autobiographical novel that documents the life of a moderately successful Trieste businessman, hilariously following his mis-steps through psychoanalysis, giving up smoking and cheating on his wife. It's a wry and very modern portrayal of procrastination, inadequacy and misadventure, and is still a terrific read today.

The plaque was installed in 1999 with the Italian ambassador in attendance. Svevo apparently settled into the neighbourhood quite well – despite calling it 'the drabbest and most out of the way suburb' – became a fan of the newly-formed Charlton Athletic, and a keen observer of working-class London society. He never really adjusted to life in Britain, however. This was chronicled in letters to his wife, Livia, recently published in *This England is So Different*, in which he talks of his struggles with the food, weather, and the London accent. What would he make of the place now? Well at least he'd be able to get a decent cup of coffee!

ENGLISH HERITAGE
Ettore Schmitz
alias
ITALO SVEVO
1861-1928
Writer
lived here
1903-1913

Address 67 Charlton Church Lane, London, SE7 7AB, www.english-heritage.org.uk/visit/ blue-plaques/ettore-schmitz | Getting there Train to Charlton; bus 53, 54 or 422 to Charlton Village, then a short walk downhill | Hours Always open | Tip You can replicate Svevo's walk to work by strolling down the hill from his house, past the turning to the football ground and across the main road, and continuing down Anchor & Hope Lane to the river. Unlike him, though, you can finish up at the excellent Anchor & Hope pub – a little-known riverside gem.

40 __ The Jetty
Totally modern concept fit for the 21st century

The Jetty's venture started in the early 2000s. From guerrilla gardening on a disused pier, it grew to become an extraordinary floating garden. In 2016, tens of thousands of salvaged plants re-homed from the RHS Chelsea Flower Show transformed it into a must-see epic landscaped garden. Now, there are seven poly-tunnels filled with diverse eye-catching plants and beds, with hundreds more outside. From the start, this project fulfilled residents' needs to connect with nature in an urban environment. At the same time, this riverside greenhouse was evolving into a multipurpose venue.

The Peninsula's burgeoning community was calling for a cultural centre on their doorstep. At first, the events were very eclectic. In 2014, The Jetty hit the headlines with its immersive theatre. Who could forget the naked man playing guitar? Then there was *The Boy Who Climbed Out of His Face* – a play in which the audience clambered barefoot through shipping containers. These days the art events are less extreme, but the schedule is regular, on-trend and often edgy. Hospitality is not limited to plants and culture: food and drinks are on offer too. The inevitable pop-up restaurant, offering burgers with seating on wooden pallets, has made way for the occasional supper-club and a more permanent coffee house.

The Jetty is a blueprint for the future of the Thames shore. Going downriver, from Enderby Wharf (see ch. 25), there are dozens of jetties and piers, many of which are unsafe and derelict. Most date back to the industrial era, when they provided a convenient platforms dedicated to the transport of heavy goods. That was the case for the Jetty site, built in the 1940s, for a coal-fired power station, but abandoned as cleaner energy gained popularity. Beside this was the old Gas Works Jetty, which now forms the base for Anthony Gormley's *Quantum Cloud* (see ch. 43). Exciting transformations indeed.

Address The Jetty, Olympian Way, London, SE10 0JF, +44 (0)20 3770 2212, www.jetty. greenwichpeninsula.co.uk | **Getting there** Tube to North Greenwich (Jubilee Line); Emirates Air Line, directly beside the cable car; bus 108, 129, 132, 161, 422, 472 or 486; by River Bus to North Greenwich Pier and walk downriver | **Hours** See website for current information on visiting | **Tip** As the jetties and piers are renovated, planning has been approved for a new floating restaurant as part of the Intercontinental Hotel, next to the O2.

41 The Laban Building

A Stirling Prize-winning arts venue

Wherever you are in the borough, you're never far from an art venue, as there's a strong tradition of music and dance. *Strictly Come Dancing*'s Len Goodman taught in the neighbourhood before launching his nearby Dance Academy in Dartford. Opened in 2001, the Laban building is a bold, iconic, and key cultural venue. It's the world's largest purpose-built contemporary dance centre, named after Austro-Hungarian choreographer Rudolf Laban, one of the founders of European Modern Dance. Designed by architects Herzog & de Meuron, also responsible for Tate Modern and the National Stadium in Beijing, the Laban building was an architectural triumph, and won the prestigious Stirling Prize, a few years later in 2003.

The soft pastel, semi-translucent walls in soothing mint, pink and lavender look stunning. During the day, their texture allows passers-by to catch glimpses of dance movement. By night, the building becomes a beacon of light – and an enchanting sight for anyone aboard a passing train. The interior doesn't disappoint either, with its 13 studios, a 300-seat theatre for live dance and music performances, and the largest dance library in Europe. Indoors, the building looks like an urban streetscape, with unconventional features such as wavy stair handrails. Not all areas are open to members of the public, who can instead book a guided tour.

This breathtaking building also provides the backdrop to impressive grounds. The grassy landscape is reminiscent of the Teletubbies' home – probably not what Vogt Landscape Architects had in mind! It is nonetheless a fitting setting for outdoor events and displays, in collaboration with the Faculty of Music based in the Old Royal Naval College compound. For two weeks every February, Trinity Laban's usual creative atmosphere gets supercharged for CoLab, an annual festival of collaboration, creativity and innovation.

Address 30 Creekside, London, SE8 3DZ, +44 (0)20 8691 8600, www.trinitylaban.ac.uk | Getting there DLR to Cutty Sark; train to Deptford; bus 188 to stop G Creekside | Hours For opening times of the café and other public areas of the building, as well as for tour schedules, visit www.trinitylaban.ac.uk/about-us/visit-us/faculty-of-dance-guided-tours | Tip The Stirling Prize is an annual award presented by the Royal Institute of British Architects (RIBA), for which North Greenwich Station, with its bold blue mosaic columns and deep blue glass wall cladding, was short-listed in 1999.

42 Lesnes Abbey

South-east London's largest historic secret

It's technically just across the border in the borough of Bexley, but Lesnes Abbey is very much a Greenwich attraction – and it is just far enough away to feel like a bit of a surprise when you stumble upon the ruins of this 12th-century building. It was founded in 1178 by one Richard de Lucy, partly as a penance for his role in the murder of Thomas à Becket in Canterbury eight years earlier. Richard was the so-called 'Chief Justiciar' at the time, a powerful post that was answerable only to the monarch. Dedicated to Saints Mary and Thomas, it housed an order of Augustinian monks who presided over all the land down to the river – now Thamesmead. This was despite the fact that it wasn't an especially large community, nor a particularly wealthy one. Rather, it served for many years as a staging post for pilgrims on the way to Canterbury – ironic, given its origins.

The reasonably substantial ruins of the abbey occupy a sweeping open space between the woods and the main road, and the plan of the church and cloister, with the refectory and monks' quarters on the far side, is clearly discernible. It was one of the first English abbeys to be dissolved under Henry VIII, ransacked and closed during the 1520s, and began to fall into ruin soon afterwards.

It's fun to clamber among the ruins before heading off into the woods beyond, where you can easily lose yourself among the ancient trees. The woods form part of a Site of Special Scientific Interest, home to fossils from the Eocene era, which can occasionally be uncovered in the sandy soil of the Fossil Pit, and in spring there are daffodils and bluebells along the old oaks, birch and chestnut trees. On the high ground just outside the woods, there's a formal viewpoint that gives an excellent view of the distant London skyline – enhanced with seats and an installation of Gothic-style arches designed to maximize the abbey vibe.

Address Abbey Road, London, SE2 0QJ | **Getting there** Train to Abbey Wood; bus 229, 469, 301 or B11 to Lesnes Abbey | **Hours** Always open | **Tip** You can explore the woods above the abbey and emerge on the far side, crossing the road to enter Bostall Woods, which you can follow through to Winns Common, then down into the mysterious gash of Slade's Ravine, before climbing back up to the Common. You can then enjoy a well-earned drink at the Old Mill – a historic pub built around an 18th-century windmill.

43___ The Line

Art walks The Line on the Peninsula

The Prime Meridian Line pops up in all sorts of unexpected places around Greenwich, crossing the tip of the Greenwich peninsula just beyond the Intercontinental Hotel. Sometimes there's a plaque or just a line, but here the route is marked by a series of roundels set into the ground to celebrate the countries along the Prime Meridian, with selections of contemporary poetry from eight of them. An extract from Poet Laureate Simon Armitage's 1,000-line Millennial poem *Killing Time* does the honours for the UK.

Beyond, the Thames Path skirts the boundary of the hotel and the O2, a stretch that's also a celebration of 'The Line' – in this case a public art walk to the Queen Elizabeth Park across the river. This starts with the crashed pylon of Alex Chinneck's *Bullet from a Shooting Star*, which evokes the stubbornly industrial landscape around. Follow the path to a decidedly more low-key work by London-based artists Jon Thomson and Alison Craighead: basically a signpost simply saying *Here, 24,859* – the length of the Prime Meridian around the earth and back. Next is Richard Wilson's *Slice of Reality* – a sliced vertical section of a sand dredger commissioned as part of the Millennium celebrations, which is both an intimate view into the bowels of an ocean-going vessel, and a rusty old reference to Greenwich's maritime history.

Further on lies Gary Hume's *Liberty Grip*, a giant bronze sculpture based on the limbs of a shop mannequin, and finally Anthony Gormley's arresting *Quantum Cloud*, set under the route of the Emirates Air Line (see ch. 24) on what's left of the original coal yards jetty, when the Peninsula was home to Europe's largest gasworks. This last sculpture, made of thousands of pieces of galvanised steel, is another Millennium piece, designed to evoke the quantum age – and a fitting symbol of the change and development taking place all around it.

Address Waterview Drive, London, SE10 0TW, www.the-line.org | Getting there Tube to North Greenwich (Jubilee Line); various buses to North Greenwich | Hours Always open | Tip Finish your visit with a trip on the Emirates Air Line (see ch. 24) and visit the other works along The Line, starting with Laura Ford's *Bird Boy* across the river.

44 Manze's Pie & Mash
London's original fast food

In the working-class neighbourhoods of east and south-east London, pie and mash shops were traditionally very common, serving what was for the best part of a century the traditional food of working folk: pies were easily transportable and filled with cheap ingredients, satisfying and filling mashed potato, and jellied eels – when the Thames was at its polluted worst, eels were basically the only kind of fish that could survive in the river's eastern reaches.

Some of the old establishments survive, one of the oldest being Manze's on Deptford High Street. Once part of a south-east London-wide chain, this is still owned and run by descendants of the original founder, Michele Manze, who arrived in the UK from southern Italy in 1878. There are also other Manze's shops in Peckham and Tower Bridge, operated by a different branch of the same family.

The Manze family were originally ice-cream makers, but soon adapted to London appetites and began offering pies and eels to the rapidly growing population of London's eastern districts. Pies and eels were the fast food of their day, being nutritious, filling, and above all easy to prepare and eat – as was the mash they were consumed with. The Manzes were one of two families that dominated the business along with the Cookes, possessing multiple shops. Those that remain still have the immaculately tiled walls, marble tables and wooden booths and benches with which they were originally furnished.

The pies themselves are made from scratch in the back of the shop, and brought through on massive trays, piping hot, to be served with a generous slab of mash. This is doused with green 'liqueur' or parsley sauce (traditionally made with a little eel water), which is then mixed with malt vinegar – although gravy is also available, if that's your preference. If there's a more historic and traditional eatery in south-east London, we've yet to hear about it.

Address 204 Deptford High Street, London, SE8 3PR, www.manze.co.uk | Getting there Train to Deptford; bus 47, 53, 187 or 453 to Deptford Broadway or 180 or 199 to Creek Road; DLR to Deptford Bridge | Hours Tue–Sat 9am–2.30pm | Tip If fish and chips is more your thing than pie and mash, you should try the Golden Chippy (62 Greenwich High Road, SE10 8LF, +44 (0)20 8692 4333). Everyone has their favourite, naturally, but this is reckoned to be one of the best in the area.

45 Maryon Wilson Park
Moody, mysterious… and maybe a murder scene?

Named after the well-to-do Maryon-Wilson family, which occupied Charlton House and owned much of the nearby land for well over a century, this park – along with the connected Maryon Park – achieved its 15 minutes of fame in the 1960s, when it was the moody backdrop to Michelangelo Antonioni's film *Blow Up*, in which David Hemmings plays a fashion photographer who believes he may have accidentally photographed a murder. It's a typically 1960s movie, slightly pretentious but extremely atmospheric, and the handsome Hemmings is the epitome of Sixties cool – something Charlton definitely wasn't at the time, and maybe still isn't!

Formerly a quarry, in part known as 'Hangman's Woods' when it hosted gibbets for captured highwaymen, Maryon Wilson Park is an enticingly wild and hilly place – a contrast to the rather flat expanse of Charlton Park across the road. It's criss-crossed by overgrown, undulating paths that still evoke the peaceful, moody feel depicted in the movie, much of which was filmed on the highest point of Maryon Park, Cox's Mount – the site, it's believed, of an ancient Roman fort.

The land was donated by the Maryon-Wilson family in 1924, and the two parks opened a couple of years later, bridging the divide between the relatively salubrious bit of Charlton at the top of the hill, near the original village, and the more industrial district at the bottom, close to the river and Woolwich's docks. Deer were introduced in the 1940s and still roam around their own enclosure at the centre of Maryon Wilson Park, across from which you can also see sheep, pigs, rabbits and other creatures (weekly guided tours). The parks also have children's playgrounds, tennis courts, a nature reserve and other activities, but really their uniqueness lies in the sense of mystery and seclusion that somehow still prevail – only occasionally disturbed by the odd film student!

Address Thorntree Road, London, SE7 8AE, www.royalgreenwich.gov.uk/directory_record/3778/maryon_wilson_park | Getting there Bus 53, 54, 380, 422 to Charlton Lane or bus 177, 180, 472 to Woolwich Road | Hours Daily 10.30am–4pm | Tip Be sure to explore Gilbert's Pit, accessible from Woolwich Road at the bottom end of Maryon Park, or from an entrance on Charlton Lane. A path effectively takes you around the rim of the original quarry, a bucolic route that feels barely in London at all – apart from the spectacular views.

46 Maze Hill Pottery
The future of pottery

In a place fashioned by history, one might not be surprised to walk along the river and see remains of the past such as broken clay pipes, locally manufactured in Plumstead, in the 1800s, by a thriving cottage industry, or fragments of pots and plates. Although such finds do occur, it might not automatically be assumed that the pottery tradition is still alive in the area – yet it is, burning bright with energy thanks to the efforts of Lisa Hammond of Maze Hill Pottery, who keeps the flame alive and the kilns hot.

Lisa's studio and her two kilns are located in an unassuming cul-de-sac, on the premises of the former railway station's ticket office. The artist has been described in *Ceramic Art Daily* as 'the best woman potter working in Britain'. The ceramicist has worked in Greenwich for the best part of 40 years, first in Royal Hill, and since 1994 in this unusual atelier. Lisa is a soda-firing potter, and her exquisite pieces are made to be handled. This is no show-gallery, it's a working studio where you'll see Lisa at her wheel throwing clay. Her calling card pieces find their roots in English medieval pots that influence her functional and tableware items intended for everyday use, and in Japanese Shino glaze pottery with decoration such as Umanome – Horse Eyes – for her personal work.

In 2016, Lisa Hammond was awarded an MBE for services to ceramics. In her own words, she is 'working for the future of pottery'. On visiting Maze Hill Pottery, you might meet one of her apprentices. Lisa has trained 14 over the past two decades. She also founded a charity called Adopt a Potter, which enables students to work alongside other master potters. And in 2017, she set up Clay College in Stoke to train 14 potters every two years. The initiative aims to curb the decline of ceramics education, and it started in Greenwich, where pottery has been alive since the 16th century.

Address The Old Ticket Office, Woodlands Park Road, London, SE10 9XE, +44 (0)20 8293 0048, www.mazehillpottery.co.uk | Getting there Train to Maze Hill, then exit via platform 2 | Hours Evening classes four times a week, open by appointment Mon–Fri 10am–6pm, and open studio once a year; check website for more info | Tip If you're interested in local arts and crafts, head for Creek Road to Made in Greenwich, a shop representing over 70 artists and craftspeople from the borough, selling wares ranging from local honey to ceramics. More info at www.madeingreenwich.shop.

47 Meantime Brewing Company

A real Greenwich success story

Arguably one of the main protagonists in the craft beer revolution, the history of Meantime Brewery is a real Greenwich success story. Founded by jobbing brewer Alistair Hook in his Greenwich flat just over 20 years ago, its growth followed the surge in interest in craft beers which continues to this day. It wasn't long before the business needed to move to larger premises on a Charlton industrial estate, afterwards setting up shop at the Old Royal Naval College's Old Brewery (see ch. 53) – brewing there for the first time in 200 years. They moved to their current, more workaday location on Blackwall Lane in 2010, which was at the time the largest brewery to be built in London since the 1930s.

Producing a range of pioneering ales, such as London Lager, IPA and Yakima Red, Hook won 'Brewer of the Year' in 2015. The business soon fell prey to the big beasts of brewing, however, and was bought for a vast sum five years ago by global giant SABMiller, who in turn sold it to the Japanese brewer, Asahi. It's now possible to buy Meantime ales pretty much anywhere in London, but Greenwich is still its home. Not only that, the pioneering spirit of brewers like Hook lives on in London: Meantime was one of just half a dozen small London breweries when it began, but there are now over 80, many of them learning their craft at Meantime.

The complex on Blackwall Lane is worth a visit for many reasons, not least its brewery shop, which sells Meantime products, occasional special edition brews that are unavailable anywhere else, and all sorts of Meantime merchandise. There's also a rather stylish bar that serves a simple menu of sides throughout the day, plus there are regular guided brewery tours that take you through the whole process.

Address Lawrence Trading Estate, Blackwall Lane, London, SE10 0AR, www.shop.
meantimebrewing.com | Getting there Train to Maze Hill; bus 188 or 422 stop right
outside | Hours Mon & Tue noon–8pm, Wed–Sat noon–10pm, Sun noon–6pm | Tip
Craft beer-lovers can also pop across the heath to the aptly named Zerodegrees in
Blackheath Village. They've been brewing their own beers on this site since 2000, and
you can enjoy them in their on-site bar and restaurant.

48 Monument to a Dead Parrot

A dead parrot?

From naval heroes to perfectly formed mermaids, Greenwich proudly celebrates its remarkable naval history and the life of its seafarers through public art. But even with all the maritime history around, it's still a little surprising to find a monument to a parrot. Especially as this bronze statue of a white cockatoo doesn't bear any resemblance to the kind of feisty bird worthy of a pirate. So why is there such a statue right in the centre of Greenwich? Sadly, nobody can provide a definitive answer, and Jon Reardon, the artist, remains silent on the subject.

We could speculate that the defunct avian, lying on his back with its little black legs in the air, is a nod to Monty Python's celebrated parrot sketch. Except that this creature is not a Norwegian blue, but a sulphur-crested cockatoo. Adding to the mystery, the words 'CHINA' are branded on its stomach. If the aim was to create a feature of interest or talking point, Jon Reardon certainly succeeded. When the bird first appeared in 2009, newspapers speculated that the Dead Parrot was intended to be the Greenwich mascot, to replace Nannie, the Cutty Sark's figurehead. Even more peculiar is the fact that the cockatoo frequently goes unnoticed, it's almost as if it had the gift of invisibility.

If you weren't actively looking for the bird, you could easily miss its white plumage on the white plinth. Indeed, when the Dead Parrot left its plinth in 2012, only the more observant residents noticed its absence. There was no outcry, certainly not on the scale of the Nelson statue or Moore's Knife Edge's incidents (see ch. 36). However, there was some concern about the whereabouts of the sculpture, and questions were asked. It transpired that the parrot had been taken to storage for the duration of the Equestrian Olympic Games, being returned safely to its perch once the horses had left town.

Address Devonport House, London, SE10 9JW, www.devere.co.uk | Getting there Boat, DLR or train to the Maritime Museum; the sculpture can be seen through the railings at the corner of King William Walk and Romney Road, or for a closer look head for De Vere Devonport hotel gardens via the National Maritime Museum | Hours All year round | Tip Greenwich Park is a great site for bird-watching. Nobody knows exactly how parakeets arrived here, but the area is home to large colonies. You'll hear them before you'll see them. Stand still by a tree and look for a flash of green overhead, or listen out for their distinctive squawk (see ch. 32).

49 Mudlarking
Treasure-hunting on the Greenwich foreshore

Greenwich is defined by the Thames, and nowhere more so than along its foreshore, where at low tide the river recedes to reveal patches of sand, pebbles and ancient jetties. These are prime locations for the ancient art of 'mudlarking' – basically searching for objects and artefacts lodged in the river mud that have been washed up by the incoming tide. It's a pastime that takes place all along the river, but for obvious reasons there are particularly rich pickings on the Greenwich stretches, where you can often spot a few figures trudging along the foreshore. To join them, you'll have to obtain a licence from the Port of London Authority and will need to follow some stringent rules, but you might just land yourself a unique souvenir.

Perhaps the most common finds on the Thames' foreshore are pieces of disposable clay pipe, which were used from the 16th century right up to Victorian times. But you could find pretty much anything in the river, which has, let's face it, been a dumping ground for all sorts for hundreds of years. Dedicated mudlarks discover bits of pottery, old bottles, even dog tags (see ch. 6). If you're really lucky you might even find an old coin from the reign of Queen Elizabeth I. There are several good spots – the area from Cutty Sark towards Deptford Creek, the stretches by the Trafalgar Tavern or Deptford Green, or the pebble beach next to Greenwich Yacht Club, for example. But be careful immediately outside the Naval College, where mudlarking is permitted but strictly monitored.

If you're planning on mudlarking there are some safety issues to consider. Novices shouldn't mudlark alone, as the tide turns fast and the mud can be hazardous. It's also advisable to wear gloves, and although mudlarking is a child-friendly activity with potential for a real living history lesson, you should keep a close eye on little ones at all times when you're by the river.

Address Along the foreshore but never east of the Thames Barrier | Getting there For mudlarking spots in central Greenwich, train to Greenwich; DLR to Cutty Sark or Greenwich; bus 129, 177, 180, 188, 199, 286 or 386 to Greenwich town centre; for Greenwich Yacht Club beach (see ch. 34), take tube to North Greenwich, or bus 129, 132, 161, 335, 472 or 486 to Millennium Village Oval Square, then walk across Ecology Park | Tip Obtain a mudlarking licence from Port of London Authority: these are easy to get and cost £90 for a year, or £40 for one visit within a given month. Visit www.pla.co.uk/Environment/Thames-foreshore-permits for more info. Thames Discovery Programme runs a year-round programme of walks and other activities exploring the archaeology of the river on the foreshore: www.thamesdiscovery.org.

50 National Maritime Museum

World's foremost collection of maritime objects

Housed in the former home of the Royal Hospital School, Greenwich's National Maritime Museum opened in 1937 and is the foremost museum of its kind in the world, with an unrivalled collection of marine and naval artefacts – more than it can show at any one time. It documents the extraordinary power and influence Britain has exerted over the past five or so centuries, from military might to trade to exploration. One visit doesn't do it justice.

The entrance hall leads to a covered central courtyard that hosts a variety of large nautical objects. Toddlers are encouraged to have an educational run around on the museum's 'Great Map of the World', while down below you might peek in to see Turner's depiction of the Battle of Trafalgar, between taking in figureheads and Prince Frederick's gilded barge from 1731. The Traders gallery has paintings depicting 17th-century Deptford, while in the 'Polar Explorers' gallery on the other side of the courtyard you can see Franklin's mittens and moccasins, and Frank Hurley's pictures of the Shackleton expedition. 'Tudors and Stuarts' includes portraits of Drake, compasses, telescopes and models of sailing vessels, while 'Nelson, Navy & Nation' contains objects relating to Britain's greatest naval hero, Lord Nelson. These include various portraits, and a famous picture depicting the admiral's death, alongside the coat he was wearing when he died at Trafalgar – the bullet-hole made by the sniper's rifle is clearly visible. It's hard to exaggerate the effect Nelson's death had on the nation: his body was brought to Greenwich, where it lay in state, for a week during a period of intense public and private grief. Perhaps most affecting, though, is the letter on display that he wrote to his daughter, Horatia, two days before his death: it begins, 'My dearest angel…'.

Address National Maritime Museum, London, SE10 9NF | **Getting there** Train to Greenwich or Maze Hill, DLR to Cutty Sark; bus 129, 177, 180, 188, 199, 286 or 386 to Greenwich town centre | **Hours** Daily 10am–5pm | **Tip** One of the Maritime Museum's most popular exhibits isn't actually in the museum at all: Yinki Shonibare's scaled-down replica of Nelson's flagship, *Victory*, complete with batik sails, is the world's largest 'ship in a bottle'. Originally exhibited in 2010 in Trafalgar Square, it sits on a plinth outside the park entrance, and is one of the area's most popular selfie sites.

51 The Naval College Chapel

Peek inside Britain's premier maritime church

It's a little overshadowed by the Painted Hall, but the Old Royal Naval College Chapel of St Peter and St Paul is no less impressive for that. It's also free, and you can pop in more or less when you feel like it.

The chapel was originally the work of Thomas Ripley, who finished the Royal Hospital complex, started by Christopher Wren, with this building, and Queen Mary Court behind, in 1751. Destroyed by fire 28 years later, it was rebuilt by James Stuart in 1789, and has remained largely unchanged since then. As a result, it's full of contemporary details, such as the large organ and the balcony on which it stands, which is a copy of the Erechtheion on the Acropolis in Athens.

It was here that the veterans worshipped, and like so much of Greenwich, it's full of maritime references. Note the rope design and 'fouled anchor' – a symbol of the admiralty – on the marble floor of the nave, and Benjamin West's enormous altarpiece, painted for this location and which depicts the shipwreck of St Paul on the isle of Malta. The curtain below is the one that screened Elizabeth II when she was secretly anointed during her 1953 coronation.

A number of memorials complete the picture of Britain's foremost maritime church, including an elaborate marble frieze in the vestibule, which commemorates John Franklin and his ill-fated expedition of the 1840s – a controversial piece that was disliked by Franklin's wife. It's also unclear which of Franklin's party lies here. Upstairs there's a bust of Nelson's right-hand man, Thomas Masterman Hardy, a much-loved governor of the Royal Hospital for many years. Hardy was known as a reformer, remembered among other things for getting rid of the practice of making Greenwich pensioners change their traditional blue coats for yellow as a mark of shame for public drunkenness. He is buried across the road in the Royal Hospital Mausoleum (see ch. 37).

Address Old Royal Naval College, London, SE10 9NN | **Getting there** Train to Greenwich or Maze Hill, DLR to Cutty Sark; bus 129, 177, 180, 188, 199, 286 or 386 to Greenwich town centre | **Hours** Daily 10am–5pm | **Tip** Perhaps the best way to experience the chapel is to attend a public performance of the Trinity Laban chapel choir here.

52 The O2

London's most popular white elephant!

If you're old enough to remember when – and why – it was built, you might remember this as the 'Millennium Dome', but it's been the O2 for years now and the name seems to have stuck. It was, however, created for the turn of the Millennium in 2000, and opened at midnight on January 1 that year with a typically British catastrophe. A flagship New Labour project, expensively designed by Richard Rogers to capture the forward-looking spirit of the nation, the trains of the brand new Jubilee line failed on its opening night, leaving hundreds of VIPs stranded in the cold and the Queen at a loose end. Not only that: the exhibition it housed for its first year was generally considered a waste of time – indeed the Dome was considered such a white elephant that when entertainment group AEG wanted to turn it into a venue, the government practically bit their hand off.

Built on the site of the old Greenwich gasworks, Greenwich Peninsula was chosen due to its auspicious place on the meridian line, but the project was a challenge from the start: the ground was poisoned with toxins and required a massive clean-up, plus it was – by London's standards – in the middle of nowhere, so the extension of the Jubilee line from across the river was essential. Arguably the Dome is more of a tent than a building, and pedants would say strictly speaking it isn't even a dome. Whatever it might be, at around £780m it was expensive, although those who know about such things say that yard-for-yard, given its enormous size, it was actually great value for money. It's certainly endured well, and its attention to detail and respect for its location at the home of time is admirable: its 365-metre diameter represents the days of the year, while 12 yellow pylons support its taut fabric roof. The Dome now not only rides high as London's premier large indoor live venue, but also as a shopping centre, with the usual chain stores, cafés and high street brands.

Address London, SE10 0DX, +44 (0)20 8463 2000, www.theo2.co.uk | Getting there Tube to North Greenwich (Jubilee Line), or various buses | Hours Daily 10am–11pm | Tip Walks across the roof of the O2 are both stimulating and popular, and run regularly throughout the year depending on the weather. You can climb during the day, at night, or even celebrate your birthday up there – visit www.theo2.co.uk/up-at-the-o2 for more info.

53__ The Old Brewery

Where Henry VIII might drink if alive today!

One of the best places to eat and drink in Greenwich – certainly among its most historic in a district where there's a fair bit of competition – The Old Brewery was founded by none other than Henry VIII, a monarch who famously loved a tipple and would probably be delighted to see that it was still going almost 500 years later. During later years the brewery was rebuilt to supply the pensioners of the Royal Naval Hospital with their regulation daily ration of three pints of ale, and was connected directly to their dining room in the Undercroft of the Queen Mary building, now the canteen of Greenwich University. If only the students of today were as pampered!

Luckily they don't have far to go: the latest incarnation of The Old Brewery is centrally placed within the Royal Naval College complex, next door to the Naval College museum and tourist information office in the Pepys Building, and it does a pretty good job of multitasking as student bar, local pub and handy pit-stop for thirsty tourists. It was empty and disused for well over a century until the turn of the Millennium, when the local Greenwich microbrewery Meantime restored it to its former glory as a brewery and tap room (see ch. 47). They did a great job, installing the copper brewing kettles in the cavernous main hall and decorating the walls with beer memorabilia. They have now left, however, leaving the long-running London real ale specialist Youngs in charge of this prime Greenwich location.

As you would expect, they serve a good selection of both draught and bottled beers along with a moderately priced menu that is deliberately full of delicious dishes that perfectly complement a glass or two of good ale – you can choose from a selection of bar snacks, sharing boards and main courses and enjoy them either in the main hall, the cosy bar, or if it's warm enough at the outside tables in and around the enclosed garden.

Address The Pepys Building, The Old Royal Naval College, London, SE10 9LW, +44 (0)20 3437 2222, www.oldbrewerygreenwich.com | Getting there Train to Greenwich or Maze Hill, DLR to Cutty Sark; bus 129, 177, 180, 188, 199, 286 or 386 to Greenwich town centre | Hours Mon–Sat 10am–11pm, Sun 10am–10pm; food served 10am–9.30pm, Sun noon–9pm | Tip Take your drink to the covered seats outside the Old Brewery's garden, and be entertained by the sounds drifting across from the Trinity School of Music opposite – a trumpet solo one minute, a perfectly delivered aria the next.

54 Old Royal Naval College
The finest architectural view in Britain?

If there is a building that defines Greenwich, it's the Royal Naval College, which dominates the riverfront and, indeed, much of the town centre. Built as Greenwich Hospital after the demolition of Henry VIII's royal palace in 1696, the architectural historian Nicholas Pevsner considered the complex the 'finest architectural view in Britain'.

Linger a while, and you can feel the weight of history: in 1714 German monarch George I arrived in Britain for the first time at the royal landing here; less than a century later, Lord Nelson's body was brought up these steps following the Battle of Trafalgar; and it was here that Queen Elizabeth II knighted a kneeling Francis Chichester after his circumnavigation of the world in 1967. And beneath your feet lie the ruins of the Greenwich Palace, birthplace of Henry VIII and his daughter Queen Elizabeth I.

A major project of King William III, Greenwich Hospital was intended as a humane retirement home for naval veterans. Christopher Wren was commissioned to design the building but he had to adhere to strict guidelines, most important of which was not to obstruct the view of the river from the Queen's House. Assisted by St Alfege architect Nichola Hawksmoor, Wren did this by constructing four quadrants around a central avenue. Sadly, he died before his vision was complete, with the final quadrant, Queen Mary Court, not completed until 1750. The first veterans took up residence in 1705, and the buildings were re-purposed as the Royal Naval College in the 1870s. This it remained until 1997, since when it has been home to the University of Greenwich and Trinity Laban School of Music and Trinity Laban School of Music and Dance. Tours start in the Pepys Building, where there's an exhibition covering the history of the site, from Tudor times to the present-day, and featuring models of the Tudor palace and Wren's replacement alongside other exhibits.

Address Old Royal Naval College, London, SE10 9NN, www.ornc.org | **Getting there** Train to Greenwich or Maze Hill, DLR to Cutty Sark; bus 129, 177, 180, 188, 199, 286 or 386 to Greenwich town centre | **Hours** Daily 10am–5pm | **Tip** Dozens of feature films have been shot in the Naval College, from *Les Misérables* to *Darkest Hour*, and you can join 'behind-the-scenes' tours of the major locations in the Naval College. These tours run on the final weekend of every month, and include the Painted Hall (see ch. 58) and Skittle Alley (see ch. 86).

55 Oliver's Jazz Bar

A classic jazz venue in almost every sense

The domain for almost two decades of genial jazz buff and sometime musician Oliver – he goes by only one name – Oliver's Jazz Club is a relatively unsung hero of the south-east London music scene. Tucked away in the basement across the street from Greenwich Theatre, you have to know it's there to find it, but once you have you'll certainly become a regular – this is a classic jazz venue in almost every sense.

Oliver is an affable Frenchman who gave up a top job in the catering industry 20 years ago to indulge his love of jazz in the best way he knew how – by creating his own venue! He couldn't have chosen a better place. Oliver's is a jazz club in the truest sense: a small, funky basement with low ceilings, a comfortable bar and a main room with a series of round tables facing a small stage. If it were still legal to smoke indoors, this would undoubtedly be the ultimate smoky jazz venue. As the *Fast Show*'s Jazz Club presenter Louis Balfour might have said: 'Nice!'

Even lacking the traditional smoky ambience, Oliver's does a pretty good job of emulating the kind of establishments the hepcats would have patronised in post-war New York, Chicago or Paris. Unsurprisingly, just a few years ago it was rated one of London's best jazz venues, hot on the heels of Ronnie Scott's.

Nothing more than an empty basement before Oliver transformed it, the venue now hosts live jazz seven nights a week. The establishment has seen some big-name performers over the years, though perhaps the most famous artist wasn't strictly jazz at all – Florence, singer with Florence and the Machine, who gigged here in her early days, when she worked at the cheese shop round the corner. The venue also regularly hosts local aspiring jazzers from the nearby Trinity Laban Music School. And who knows, if you ply Oliver with a drink or two, he might even get out his blues harp and do a turn himself.

Address 9 Nevada Street, London, SE10 9JL, +44 (0)20 8858 3693, www.oliversjazzbar.com |
Getting there Train to Greenwich or Maze Hill, DLR to Cutty Sark; bus 129, 177, 180, 188,
199, 286 or 386 to Greenwich town centre | Hours Bar opens at 4pm daily, with live music
9pm – midnight (Sun 5 – 8pm) | Tip Other intimate venues in central Greenwich include the
popular Argentinian restaurant Buenos Aires Café, around the corner from Oliver's and worth
a visit for its food too, and the Prince of Greenwich, a five-minute walk away on Royal Hill,
also worth a visit for its food. Both host music weekly.

56 Our Ladye Star of the Sea

Classic Victorian Gothic part-decorated by Pugin

Built as an act of thanks in the middle of the 19th century, the church of Our Ladye Star of the Sea occupies its place half-way up Crooms Hill with considerable grace. This impressive, spired, neo-Gothic church was designed and built by William Wardell according to the principles of the prolific Catholic architect August Pugin.

It's both a statement and a place of worship, and was originally funded in part by the North family, in gratitude for the rescue of their sons following a boating accident on the river. The North sons both became priests and served in the local Catholic mission, and are now laid to rest within the church.

Our Ladye Star of the Sea was a replacement for a tiny chapel on Park Vista, which during the first half of the 19th century was Greenwich's only Catholic place of worship. Much of the interior decoration was designed by Pugin himself, and thus the church is of considerable interest to scholars of the period. A staunch Catholic convert, Pugin built Gothic Revival churches all over the country, with his distinctive throwback style culminating in the mock medieval grandeur of the Houses of Parliament.

Inside, the church is a classic Victorian Gothic structure, with a nave divided by Gothic arches, a stone carved rood screen, and statue of the Virgin supported by the Old Testament figures of Ruth, Esther and Judith (clasping the head of Holofernes). Indeed, the church is a feast of carvings and sculptures, angels and intimate chapels, all of which is certain have made the church's cosmopolitan congregation of sailors from Ireland, Portugal and elsewhere feel right at home. The Chapel of the 'Blessed Sacrament' is a stand-out feature, as is the Ladye Chapel, both of which are the work of Pugin himself – much to the disgust of Wardell, with whom he is said to have had a notoriously fractious relationship.

Address 68 Crooms Hill, London, SE10 8HG | **Getting there** Bus 53 or 386, then a short downhill walk; train to Greenwich; bus to Greenwich town centre, then a short uphill walk | **Hours** Tue–Fri 9.30–10.30am, Sat 10–11am & 6–7pm, Sun 9–10am & 11am–noon | **Tip** Stroll down the hill and you'll reach another historic building: an elegant brick Gazebo built in 1672 for the Lord Mayor of London, who lived in the house behind. You can't go in, but like the interior of the church, its pyramidal roof strikes an almost Italian note among Crooms Hill's largely Georgian buildings.

57 Oxleas Woodlands

Pleasant walks now, but not always the case

Nowadays Shooters Hill Road conjures up visions of endless traffic jams flanked on both sides by large grey and tired houses – an outward place with various facilities but no centre. There was a time when Shooters Hill meant prosperity and gentry, however. Back in the 19th century, the Hill was a desirable postcode. Being the highest point in London at 129 metres, the hill offered then, as now, magnificent views over the city. Captains of industry, shipbuilders and landowners all aspired to dwell in one of these mansions. Ironically, it was free of pollution, and clear of the thick fog that plagued London. This balloon of oxygen was magnified by the proximity of large woods.

Oxleas Wood is at least 8,000 years old, one of very few remaining areas of ancient forest. It encompasses 130 hectares of woodland and meadow, over half of which has been identified as a Site of Specific Scientific Interest (SSSI). It's home to a wide range of wildlife, including spotted and green woodpeckers. On summer evenings bats can be seen hunting too. The woods have well-defined footpaths, perfect for walking, and it's part of the London Green Chain walk: 50 miles of untouched and protected land. The Friends of Oxleas Woodlands have restored the historic rose gardens in Castle Wood according to the original planting scheme.

These days the woods are a haven of tranquillity, but that hasn't always been the case, as highwaymen and other cutpurses operated in the area for centuries. This wasn't a safe place to cross on your way to Dover. The area was very convenient for ambushing stage-coaches despite the gibbets erected along the way to remind thieves of their fate if caught. 18th-century thieves were so cocky that they dropped threatening notes on Blackheath warning folks that if they were caught travelling in the area without 10 shillings, they'd be stripped and beaten 'very heartily'.

Address Crown Woods Lane, London, SE18 3JA, www.oxleaswoodlands.uk | Getting there Bus 89, 244, 486 or B16 all pass nearby and stop at the Red Lion | Tip Within the wood there's a large and thriving honeybee apiary, and honey is for sale at the café.

58 The Painted Hall

London's Sistine Chapel

The crowning glory of the Old Royal Naval College is also its best-known feature, the Painted Hall, which occupies one of the two domed wings at the heart of the complex. Designed as the refectory of the Greenwich pensioners, it was finished in 1705. Imposing by any standards, its painted ceiling is considered one of the great artworks of the English Baroque period: a swirling, drama-crammed homage to British naval power that was such a hit when unveiled in 1714 that the pensioners were relegated to the undercroft below – now the site of the café and shop.

The painting is the work of James Thornhill, and took 19 years to complete. Thornhill wasn't the best-known artist of his day, but he was a loyal Protestant and, perhaps most importantly, came relatively cheap; he was paid just £6000, including expenses for a work that took the best years of his working life. We should be happy he took the job – his Painted Hall is a magnificent achievement.

Known as Britain's Sistine Chapel, it's a busy painting, with around 200 figures crowded into a 15x30 metres space. Like Michelangelo's more celebrated work, the narrative and symbolism are clear. Centre stage are William and Mary, the monarch's boot in the downtrodden face of the French king; there's a sailing ship at each end, one a captured Spanish galleon, the other HMS *Blenheim,* in commemoration of a famous naval victory of 1704. On the upper level, a plaque marks the spot where Nelson's coffin lay in state, below a very grand family portrait of George I, which includes everyone except his wife Sophia Dorothea, whom he imprisoned for over 30 years after her adultery. Thornhill cheekily painted himself into the picture, holding out his hand as if asking for more money. He shouldn't really have complained: he was knighted for his efforts in 1720, and later landed a prime job contributing to the decoration of St Paul's Cathedral.

Address Old Royal Naval College, London, SE10 9NN | Getting there Train to Greenwich or Maze Hill; DLR to Cutty Sark; bus 129, 177, 180, 188, 199, 286 or 386 to Greenwich town centre | Hours Daily 10am–5pm | Tip Thornhill's ceiling is full of small as well as large details: notice in the south-east corner, for example, a portrait of John Flamsteed, the first Astronomer Royal, and for that reason alone as great a symbol of Britain's global superiority as any naval hero.

59__Paul Rhodes Bakery

It's official: Rhodes makes Britain's best loaf

Master-crafted breads and lovingly presented patisseries are not easy to come by. Despite the recent bread-making revival, artisan bakeries are still few and far between. In this context, the presence of a bakery-patisserie in the centre of Greenwich, led by a passionate baker with no less than three Michelin stars, is noteworthy. Founded in 2003 by Chef Paul Rhodes, this corner shop has become one of the top go-to suppliers of quality handcrafted loaves, cakes and pastries in London. The bakery is difficult to miss with its imposing mauve awning and glass frontage. Seating is limited, but with the benches on the river-front only a couple of minutes away, this is more of an opportunity than a hindrance.

Paul Rhodes grew up in a family of hoteliers, so his career choice was almost made for him. He trained under the legendary French chef, Pierre Koffmann, at La Tante Claire, and later went on to secure a third star for Nico Ladenis' restaurant Chez Nico. In 2018, he won the British Baker of the Year Award.

Rhodes has a rare approach to making bread. His range is handcrafted with predominantly British-grown grains that reduce imported ingredients. With his team, he spent a lot of time working with British farmers and millers to source and produce new breads with traditional techniques. Who could resist his sourdough range? You have to get to the bakery early to get a Heritage or Sicilian Olive Sourdough loaf, and the slowly fermented emmer loaves fly off the shelves too.

Rhodes is now part and parcel of Greenwich scenery, and it's not unusual to see the familiar mauve-signature vehicles among the traffic in the area. The bakery supplies major hotels, restaurants, bars and delis throughout the capital. Boxes are delivered locally too, and of course, everyone passing through the centre can pick up a citron tart or chocolate brownie, gooey to perfection.

Address 37 King William Walk, London, SE10 9HU, +44 (0)20 8858 8995, www.rhodesbakery.co.uk | Getting there DLR to Cutty Sark; train to Greenwich; boat, MBNA Thames Clippers depart from all major London piers every 20 minutes; bus 53, 54, 129, 177, 180, 188, 199, 202, 286, 380, 386 or N1 to Cutty Sark | Hours Daily 7am – 6pm | Tip Straddling the border of the boroughs of Greenwich and Lewisham, you'll find the Blackheath Standard area, which is host to another artisan-baker: Boulangerie Jade, owned by *Bake Off: The Professionals* finalist, Christophe Le Tynevez-Dobel (see also ch. 77). Croque-en-Bouche, anyone?

60_ The Pelton Arms

A pub with two names

In the early 1800s, East Greenwich and The Peninsula were known as Bendish Marsh. The area was mostly pasture, marshes, some heavy industries and... The Pelton Arms. Change was on its way, however. In 1838, Coles Child, a coal merchant from County Durham, took out a lease on The Great Meadow. As demand for coal, tar, cement and other heavy industrial goods grew, so did the immediate area. New streets appeared, all named by Coles Child after the collieries of his native north: Caradoc, Braddyll, Whitworth, and of course Pelton Road. Terraced cottages for dock workers and their families were built, and sold at auctions which took place, where else, but at The Pelton Arms. By now, the pub was a hub for the area.

The pub's exterior has changed little since its beginnings. It's retained the Victorian frontage typical of many London pubs of the area. Dark green glazed tiles and gold lettering give it a very traditional look. Downstairs, there's an L-shaped bar with an eclectic variety of seating from wooden tables, benches and stools, to comfy well-loved sofas. A mixture of lights, including a granny floor lamp, as well as historic photographs, all give the rooms a warm, homely feeling. Upstairs there are a few rooms for visitors. There's a secluded garden and real ales, bar billiards, a dartboard, and friendly staff ensure return visitors.

Don't be fooled by appearances, though: The Pelton Arms is very much a one-off. In 2010, the pub appeared in *Rock and Chips*, the prequel to *Only Fools and Horses*, where it became the 'Nag's Head', hence the two different names on each side of the façade. But its main claim to fame is the live music scene. The Pelton Arms has played host to many bands over the years. It's renowned for showcasing some of the best bands in South East London; famously the rock-band Squeeze played a gig here. Yet despite all the famous links, The Pelton Arm remains very much a local hub.

Address 23-25 Pelton Road, London, SE10 9PQ, +44 (0)20 8858 0572, www.peltonarms.com | Getting there Tube to North Greenwich (Jubilee Line), then bus 188 or 422 to Tyler Street; train to Maze Hill | Hours Mon – Thu 2pm – midnight, Fri – Sun noon – midnight | Tip If you fancy a curry after visiting the Pelton Arms, the nearby Mountain Views – a Nepalese Restaurant – 160 Trafalgar Road – is the place to go to.

61   Peninsula Square
City life perfected!

Greenwich Peninsula doesn't really have a centre, but if it did it would be Peninsula Square – a triangular open space that has evolved over the past few years into something resembling a proper urban hub. The first buildings here were the tube station and the O2, but they have since been joined by a handful of restaurants, cafés and shops. These days there's an energy about the place that didn't exist a decade ago, with strollers, sightseers, commuters and curious folk wandering into the O2 to see the shops and restaurants by day or catching a show after dark. The scattering of seats only adds to the air of city life lived well, and when the deliberately densely built shops, housing and workshops of the so-called 'Design District' on the southern side is completed, it will undoubtedly feel like a proper little urban paradise.

The far side of the square is marked by a 45-metre stainless Peninsula Spire – a graceful, twisting pinnacle that was the UK's tallest steel sculpture when it was erected in 2006. Beyond here, it's possible to ascend – either by steps or lift – to The Tide, a brand-new elevated walkway and park. This leads past the Liquorice Allsorts-style swirls of the Ravensbourne Art College building towards the river, taking in an assortment of miniature fir trees and plants, with with a selection of seating and artworks along the way.

Intended eventually to stretch for five kilometres, The Tide was conceived by the same designers as Manhattan's successful 'High Line', and it makes a nice spot to sit and linger, watching the river go by or inspecting Damien Hirst's large and flamboyant *Mermaid* sculpture on the far side. Hirst used to live on the Peninsula – in one of the old watermen's cottages next to The Pilot pub (see ch. 64) – and the *Mermaid* was featured in his 2017 Venice exhibition, *Treasures from the Wreck of the Unbelievable*. Other permanent works here include veteran pop artist Allen Jones' big red steel sculpture, *Head in the Wind*.

Address Peninsula Square, London, SE10 0AX | **Getting there** Tube to North Greenwich (Jubilee Line); Emirates Air Line Cable Car from East London; various buses | **Hours** Always open | **Tip** One of Greenwich Peninsula's most visible landmarks is the 49-metre tower of sculpted triangles of the Low Carbon Energy Centre, whose hi-tech, planet-friendly boilers provide power for the homes and offices of the Peninsula – the tower is the flue. Designed by Conrad Shawcross, the panels aim to create a 'Moiré Effect' of overlapping patterns, and at night are illuminated to dramatic effect. The visitor centre inside provides more info.

62 Peter the Great Monument

One of the weirdest statues in Britain!

When Peter the Great arrived in Deptford in 1698, the Royal Dock-yard was the most important of its kind in England. The Tzar of Russia came here to learn shipbuilding. Although he stayed only a short time, his visit was nonetheless eventful: during his four months at Sayes Court in Sir John Evelyn's home (see ch. 82), he not only ruined the house, but also destroyed a precious holly bush, which was flattened by a wheelbarrow whilst the drunken Tzar was sitting in it!

Deptford dockyard closed in 1869. To commemorate the tercentenary of the Tzar's visit, the Russian people gifted Deptford a very odd-looking monument: a bronze statue by Mihail Chemiakin. The sculptor's work can be seen in New York, Venice and Paris, and his pieces are known for featuring a fair number of odd creatures – and Deptford's is no exception. This particular statue looks on to the Thames, and depicts the Tzar, a court dwarf, a throne, and a couple of cannons. Court dwarfs were favoured by the Tzar, but this one is strangely proportioned, being half the size of a small person, whilst Peter is twice his normal size – apart from his head, which is tiny. Peter wears a ruffled garment and a highly decorated tricorn, while the dwarf is adorned with lovely laced clothes and a top hat. A cherub flautist sits on his shoulder, and he holds an armillary astrolabe plus a tiny ship.

Although highly decorated, the seat looks almost as it should – apart from the myriad of ears adorning the back. There is so much to see that it would be easy to miss the plinth, whose equally wacky panels depict food and drink. On the Tzar's left-hand side is an empty throne, which makes a good spot for selfies. The artist's original intention was to have several dwarves baring their buttocks, but that was not to be. And it's not something we'd advise when taking that selfie…

Address 33 Glaisher Street, London, SE8 3ER – between Greenfell Mansions and the river |
Getting there Walk or cycle along the river bank – the statue is next to the suspension
bridge; bus 108, 188, 199, N1 or N199 to Z/Creekside | Hours The public path beside the
river is open 24/7 throughout the year | Tip The two cannons included in the statue are very
decorative. The royal borough has long been associated with gun foundry. The Royal Brass
Foundry was built in 1717 in Woolwich. The impressive building situated at No1 Street,
London, SE18 6GH has tall doors to allow the transfer of newly-made cannons.

63 Peter Harrison Planetarium

Celestial calculations to make your head spin

It's a curious fact that one of Greenwich Royal Observatory's most popular attractions is in fact underground – the 120-seat Peter Harrison Planetarium. This scientific attraction has hosted regular astronomy shows since it opened in 2007. Situated beneath a blunt cone, it's London's only Planetarium, and stands in the observatory grounds mid-way between the older buildings of the original observatory and its Victorian extension – the South Building.

The 'cone' resonates with the sort of astronomical and celestial calculations that will make your head spin, but which are nonetheless pertinent to its location. It's tilted at precisely 51.5 degrees – Greenwich's latitude – and the angle points directly to the north star. Meanwhile, the top is angled in a precise relationship with the equator. Clad with no less than 250 pieces of phosphor bronze, it also represents one of the largest single uses of bronze in the world.

The entrance to the Planetarium is through the South Building. This was built at the end of the 19th century to accommodate the Lassell Telescope, and now houses exhibition spaces, a shop and a café. A closer look at the cornice above the entrance reveals the names of no less than 24 historical Greenwich figures, starting with the first Astronomer Royal, John Flamsteed. Inside the planetarium's auditorium, the seats swing back so audiences can comfortably take in the shows projected onto its domed ceiling, through a fish-eye lens using red, green and blue lasers. The shows vary from journeys through the Solar System to sci-fi epics, and even lectures from eminent astrophysicists. It's sometimes possible to see live events streamed from the Altazimuth Pavilion, which houses an exhibition about the sun, as well as the fabulous digital Annie Mauder Astrographic telescope, installed in 2017.

Address Blackheath Avenue, London, SE10 8XJ, +44 (0)20 8312 6608 | Getting there Train to Greenwich or Maze Hill, DLR to Cutty Sark or Greenwich; bus 129, 177, 180, 188, 199, 286 or 386 to Greenwich town centre | Hours Daily 10am–5pm | Tip The only free parts of the Royal Observatory are the astronomical galleries in the South Building, where the stand-out exhibit is a chunk of the Gibeon meteorite, which crashed to Earth in the 19th century in what is now Namibia. At 4.5 billion years, it's the oldest thing you're likely to see, formed about the same time as the Earth.

64 __ The Pilot

Historic inn that's a Britpop landmark

If you're old enough, and a music fan, cast your mind back to the years of Cool Britannia, when a row of workers' cottages next door to this ancient pub featured in Blur's video for their hit song *Park Life* in 1994. The cottages and pub look much the same today as they did then, when they were also briefly home to one Damien Hirst in the days before he gained notoriety as one of Britain's cutting-edge young artists. Since then, with the construction of the Millennium Dome and North Greenwich tube station, the area has changed almost beyond recognition, and The Pilot is almost a village pub again.

In the days before Britpop, The Pilot was a watering-hole for the workers of the peninsula, who loaded coal at nearby jetties. Some of them lived in the terrace of cottages, which, like the pub, dates back to 1801, and has been mercifully preserved. It's claimed that the land around was owned by William Pitt the Younger, with the name of the pub referring to 'the pilot who weathered the storm', as Pitt was known in a popular song of the time. The street itself, now known as River Way because it once led down to the river, was formerly called 'Ceylon Place' – as recorded by a stone tablet set into the pub's wall.

An elegant Georgian building, the pub has naturally changed somewhat over the last 200 years, but retains the feel of a local neighbourhood boozer, even in the shadow of the looming skyscrapers. It serves good food and has some cosy rooms upstairs for those seeking an alternative to the charms of the nearby Holiday Inn. Owned and run by Fullers, it remains a homely and characterful establishment, with lots of nooks and crannies, and a terrace and garden out the back. It's a perfect place to stop off when visiting the O2 (see ch. 52), just a 10-minute walk away, and the Emirates Air Line Cable Car (see ch. 24), which transports you across the river to the Royal Victoria Dock and Excel Centre in the most scenic way possible.

Address 68 River Way, London, SE10 0BE | **Getting there** Tube to North Greenwich (Jubilee Line); bus 108, 161, 199, 335, 422 or 472 | **Hours** Mon–Sat 11am–11pm, Sun noon–10.30pm | **Tip** Riverway used to lead to a spot on the Thames known as 'Bugsby's Hole', where the unfortunates who had been executed on the Peninsula (its northern tip was a popular place of execution) were 'gibbeted', that is displayed to the public – presumably as a deterrent. While there are references to a 'Bugsby' all over this area, no one knows who he was, although there's a possibility it's derived from the 'bugs', 'bogeys' or 'ghouls' that would have undoubtedly haunted such a gruesome place.

65 __ The Plume of Feathers

An old-time local favourite

A pub crawl in the borough will take weeks, so best tackle the challenge in chronological order, starting with The Plume of Feathers, the oldest public house in Greenwich, dating back to 1691. When this tavern first opened, there were chickens in the courtyard and Park Vista was a busy road leading to Dover. Known at the time as the 'Prince of Wales', it was around 1720 that the landlady renamed it The Plume of Feathers, after the heraldic badge of the Prince of Wales. It's still family-run, with a mother and son team at the helm. Susan Rose has been behind the bar since 1980, ensuring that The Plume of Feathers remains a constant in our fast-changing world. Its warm atmosphere will lure you in, its quiet charm will put you at ease, and you probably won't want to leave.

Only a few minutes away from the royal park and almost on the Meridian Line, this is the first pub in the eastern hemisphere, and a prime selfie spot. The Line is just outside, there's a plaque on the wall opposite, and silver studs on the street. One would think that such a place would be busy with tourists, but this isn't yet the case. Visitors are more than welcomed, but The Plume of Feathers is a true local, firmly rooted in the area. Here, you get a consistently good pint of draught beer, typically Adnams, Harvey's Sussex Best Bitter, and another couple of guest beverages. Its original Claygate fireplace and cosy interior, and the constant soft hubbub of conversations, provide a country-pub feeling, while at the back there's a restaurant leading to a very pleasant beer garden – perfect for families with its toy house.

As a bonus, the walls feature maritime memorabilia, historical paintings and an original newspaper clipping of the battle of Trafalgar, telling many stories of Greenwich's past. In fact Lord Nelson used to meet Lady Hamilton here, when she lived next door, now renamed Hamilton House.

Address 19 Park Vista, London, SE10 9LZ, +44 (0)20 8858 1661, www.plumeoffeathers-greenwich.co.uk | **Getting there** Train to Maze Hill, DLR to Cutty Sark; tube to North Greenwich (Jubilee Line), then bus 129 or 188; bus 129, 177, 188, 236, 326 | **Hours** Mon–Thu noon–11pm, Fri noon–midnight, Sat 11am–midnight, Sun 11am–midnight | **Tip** The Pagan fertility god Herne the Hunter/the Green Man was one of the main gods of the ancient Briton. A carving of a head that resembles the Green Man can be found above an old entrance to 37 Park Vista opposite the pub.

66 The Prime Meridian

Where east meets west, follow the line

An imaginary line that divides East from West, the Prime Meridian centres on Greenwich, which at Zero Degrees Longitude is the point from which all time is measured. Why Greenwich? Well, very simply because measuring Longitude was a problem that had foxed many of the world's greatest minds for generations, but in 1765 it was finally solved when Greenwich clockmaker John Harrison devised a series of portable clocks that were accurate to within a few seconds, even at sea – transforming the art of navigation and securing Greenwich's place in history – and geography – forever.

The rotation of the Earth and its position in relation to the sun, mean that there is a crucial relationship between longitude and time. Before the 1840s, people used to get the time from churches or sundials, which was fine as most people moved around very little. But for seafaring nations like Britain time-keeping was a real problem: seafarers had no way of pinpointing their exact location, Magellan 'lost' a whole day going around the Earth and the advent of rail travel just made things worse. With improvements in rapid communication and travel, constant time-keeping became vital, and 'Greenwich Mean Time' was finally adopted in the UK in 1880.

No wonder, then, that millions of annual visitors stand with a foot on either side of the golden line at the Observatory. In the 21st century this is where #PrimeMeridian Instagram selfies have to be taken, but you'll also find it marked by a sundial in the park and at the aptly-named Meridian Lounge of the InterContinental Hotel; several schools chose to make a feature of it, including Meridian Primary School which marks the line in the playground and classrooms; a blue line cuts through the otherwise green tennis courts of Greenwich Park; while at night a green laser marks it in the sky from the observatory – a real spectacle when it rains.

Address The Royal Observatory is located in Greenwich Park, Blackheath Avenue, London, SE10 8XJ | Getting there Car parking is available for visitors with disabilities only; limited pre-booked spaces are available via bookings@rmg.co.uk; the Royal Observatory is at the top of a fairly steep hill; allow 15 minutes on foot from King William Walk; DLR or boat to Cutty Sark; train to Maze Hill or Blackheath, then a 20-minute flat walk across the heath | Hours Wed–Sun 10am–4pm | Tip On the Thames Path behind the O2, between branches of the Blackwall Tunnel, you'll find a sign showing the distance from Waterloo station in one direction and the Thames Barrier in the other, but more importantly, it's positioned right on the Meridian line.

67 __ The Prince of Greenwich

The perfect local boozer – run by Italians!

One of a trio of pubs a few minutes away from the centre of Greenwich on Royal Hill, among the residential streets of West Greenwich, the Prince of Greenwich is the latest incarnation of a pub that was formerly known as the Prince Albert – a resolutely ungentrified watering-hole that was mainly known for its dart boards and pool tables. Not a bad place, then, but one that hadn't changed for years, until Pietro la Rosa arrived from Brazil with his family five years ago to put their own unique stamp on the place.

What a difference they have made! The Albert may have gone, but the Prince of Greenwich is a fantastic replacement, catapulting the pub into the 21st century while retaining the essential Victorian 'pubiness' of the establishment. Indeed, if anything, this has been enhanced, with Pietro's fascinating collection of antiques, statues, rhino heads, masks and models and other bits and bobs filling every nook and cranny of the downstairs bar, all of which make it easy to feel immediately at home. That and the warm southern Italian welcome that you encounter behind the bar.

Not only has the Prince of Greenwich been reinvented, it's no off-the-shelf fake, but a proper pub, run by a landlord who has been warmly embraced by the local community, one of whom even painted the portrait of Pietro that adorns the pub sign outside. Most importantly, it now serves excellent Italian food on a regularly changing menu: homemade pasta, great pizzas and usually a handful of Sicilian meat and fish dishes – nothing fancy, just the sort of food you'd be more than happy to be served in downtown Palermo. Add to this the fact that they have a terrific upstairs room and host live music, and even a weekly film club, and you have in many ways the ideal local boozer. So if, like me, two of your favourite things in life are pubs and the food of Italy, this might be just the place!

Address 72 Royal Hill, London, SE10 8RT, www.theprinceofgreenwichpub.com | Getting there Train or DLR to Greenwich; bus 177, 180, 199 or 386 to the bottom of Royal Hill | Hours Mon–Thu 4–11pm, Fri 4–11.30pm, Sat noon–11.30pm, Sun noon–10.30pm | Tip Pietro and his family – Paola, Margherita and Rosita – offer free Italian conversation classes and can also facilitate trips to Sicily. Just ask them for details!

68 Queen Caroline's Bath
Royal scandals and pool parties

Near Chesterfield Gate at the top end of Greenwich Park, hidden behind a thick hedge, lie the remains of a plunge pool used by Queen Caroline, estranged wife of George IV. Many reported rowdy stories are linked to this unassuming structure!

Bathhouses were popular in Georgian times, usually located near a source of water, away from the main buildings. The water was cold, and bathers remained clothed throughout their dip. Queen Caroline's plunge pool was different, however, as it was attached to her residence. You can still see where the windows were blocked off to become part of Greenwich Park's wall. The sunken bath would have been enclosed in a glass structure with an adjoining greenhouse. The steps leading down to the pool are intact, and although the tiles are in disrepair, their original baby-blue colour is still visible.

Caroline, Princess of Brunswick, arrived in London in 1795 to marry her cousin, George. This marriage of convenience was intended to bring a much-needed fortune to the future King, who was famous for his somewhat overindulgent lifestyle. It was dislike at first sight, however, as George considered the princess ugly and 'unhygienic'. Despite this, Princess Charlotte was born a year later, although soon after George and Caroline separated. Caroline moved to Montague House in Blackheath where she entertained London high-society. The place was famous for its wild parties, and it was rumoured that fun-loving Caroline had many liaisons. There were even rumours of orgies, and an illegitimate child. A Royal Commission proved nothing, and she was cleared of adultery. In 1814, Caroline moved to Italy. As soon as she'd gone, George, now Prince Regent, ordered Montague house to be razed to the ground. The sunken bath escaped due to its underground location. It remained hidden beneath flower beds until 1909, when it was rediscovered, being fully excavated in 2001.

Address Chesterfield Gate, Greenwich Park, London, SE10 8QY | **Getting there** Bus 53 or 386 to Chesterfield Gate/Greenwich Park; 25-minute walk from Greenwich town centre, following signs for the Rose Garden | **Hours** Daily 6am–6pm (hours vary by season) | **Tip** Caroline of Brunswick was appointed Park Ranger in 1806. The Ranger's House, situated next to the remains of Caroline's bath, hosts the wonderful Wernher Collection (see ch.72).

69 Queen Elizabeth's Oak

Ancient tree that sheltered Elizabeth I as a child

As the former royal hunting grounds of Henry VIII, and one of London's eight royal parks, Greenwich Park is littered with bits and pieces pertaining to the monarchy. Perhaps the oldest is known as Queen Elizabeth's Oak, which you'll find just a three-minute walk from the Royal Observatory, not far from one of the park's Maze Hill gates. The tree is remarkable mainly for its age – it's estimated to date back to the late 13th century – and the fact that it's pretty much the most intact remnant of Greenwich's Tudor heyday. Those expecting a vigorous, upright tree will be disappointed, however: the oak has been dead for over a hundred years, and having been supported by ivy, it finally toppled over in 1991, and now lies on its side – a rather undignified wooden shell coated with various varieties of forest fungus.

The tree is believed to have already been around 400 years old and in its prime, when Elizabeth was alive, and it's claimed that Henry VIII once danced around the tree with Elizabeth I's mother, Anne Boleyn – though that could be an apocryphal story. What's not in doubt, however, is that Elizabeth was born in the palace at Greenwich in 1533, and used to take shelter here as a child when riding in the grounds of the palace. It's thought to have died around the mid-to-late 19th century, after which its hollow trunk was furnished with a door, and used to detain local villains and those who broke the rules of the park.

Unfortunately, it's not possible to have your picnic on the trunk or even get close to the tree, due to the railings that now surround it. There's an information board and a more recent oak tree stands just beside it, though, a sapling planted in 1992 by the Duke of Edinburgh to mark the Queen's ruby jubilee, which one day will no doubt grow to become just as magnificent as its 13th-century predecessor. For the moment, enjoy the park's many other veteran trees, many of which were planted in the 17th century by Charles II (see ch. 104).

Address Greenwich Park, London, SE10 9NN, www.royalparks.org.uk/parks/greenwich-park | **Getting there** Train to Greenwich or Maze Hill; DLR to Cutty Sark; bus 129, 177, 180, 188, 199, 286 or 386 to Greenwich town centre | **Hours** See website for current information on visiting | **Tip** Stroll down to the Queen's House to see the gallery of Tudor portraits, including Elizabeth and Henry.

70__ The Queen's House
Inigo Jones' first masterpiece

The elegant centrepiece of Greenwich's grand ensemble of buildings, which stretches down from the Greenwich Park Observatory to the Royal Naval College, the Queen's House is a refined Palladian palace. The work of Inigo Jones, who designed it in 1616, following numerous trips to Italy, it's perhaps the first properly classical structure in the country. It was originally built for Anne of Denmark, wife of James I, but she in fact spent hardly any time here. The house passed to the French wife of Charles I, Henrietta Maria, who finished it, and lived here on and off from 1625 until the Civil War.

Linked to the buildings of the neighbouring Maritime Museum by covered colonnades, the house was decorated by some of Europe's finest artists, and would have been one of the most precious artistic sights in the country if these hadn't been lost. Even without them, it's impressive. The central Great Hall rises to the height of both floors, a perfect cube that emphasises the building's understated elegance and proportions. Its ceiling was formerly home to a series of paintings by Orazio Gentileschi (helped by his daughter Artemisia) but these were moved to Marlborough House, where they remain. The panels now display an illustrative work in gold leaf by the British contemporary artist Richard Wright.

Most of the upstairs apartments are given over to showing some of the Maritime Museum's paintings – worth seeing even if you have no interest in the house, not least the powerful and iconic 'Armada Portrait' of Elizabeth 1, along with various depictions of the other Tudor monarchs. There are views of Greenwich by Caneletto and Turner, portraits of Queen Anne and her fellow Stuarts, and a Van Dijk marital portrait of Daniel Mytens – his predecessor as court artist to Charles I – in a setting that really couldn't be better. What a pity the original works aren't here too!

Address Romney Road, London, SE10 9NF, +44 (0)20 8858 4422 | **Getting there** Train to Greenwich or Maze Hill; DLR to Cutty Sark; bus 129, 177, 180, 188, 199, 286 or 386 to Greenwich town centre | **Hours** Daily 10.30am–4pm | **Tip** Don't miss the gorgeous curved Tulip Stairs off one corner of the Great Hall, which is famously haunted by a shrouded figure – photographed in 1966 by a Canadian tourist and since seen (and its presence felt) by various gallery assistants and other visitors.

71_ The Queen's Orchard

A feast for the eyes, an inspiration for gardeners

Until 1889, Greenwich was in Kent, and orchards were plentiful. While only a few remain, none are as idyllic as the Queen's Orchard, a genuine horticultural gem. Dating back four centuries, it has an interesting history. It's mentioned by name on documents and maps dating back to 1693. By then, it had already been enclosed within Greenwich Park walls. It's likely the orchard was used for the production of food for the Queen's House, which was completed around 1636 for Henrietta Maria, wife of Charles I. During World War II, the plot was turned into an allotment, and in 1970 locals campaigned to prevent a block of flats being built upon it. The space was then bought by Greenwich Council, and left wild until it was transferred to Greenwich Park in 2007. Friends of the Park contributed to its restoration, turning it into an inspirational garden.

Visitors gain access through a highly decorative gate designed by local artist Heather Burrell. During the restoration work, a digger stumbled into a large hole near the entrance, which proved to be an ice well – a fridge for wealthy Victorians. Besides flowers and vegetables, the orchard contains a large number of fruit trees, including apple, pear, plum, cherry, peach, nectarine, apricot, quince and medlar. Some are heritage varieties dating back to the 1500s. The veteran black mulberry tree was planted between 1607 and 1612, one of many such trees that were part of James I's Greenwich mulberry plantations for his silk project, as the king had eyes on the Western silk industry (see ch. 10). However, if silk worms thrive on white mulberry, they find the black variety less appealing, resulting in a lower yield.

While King James' silk scheme was not a success, only one garnment was ever made, the same can't be said for the lovely Queen's Orchard. Since re-opening it has become a popular corner of the park, thanks to the dedication of the volunteers who care for it.

Address The Queen's Orchard is located in the north-east corner of Greenwich Park, near the children's playground, to the right of the Maze Hill entrance. | **Getting there** Train to Maze Hill; bus 129, 177, 180 or 386 to Maze Hill bus stop G | **Hours** Wed–Fri 10.45am–4.45pm (closed for lunch 1–2pm); weekends & bank holidays, 9.15am–4.45pm; closed 1 Nov–Easter; guide dogs only | **Tip** Running along the boundary of Queen's House in Greenwich Park is the longest herbaceous border in London, measuring 200 metres. It was planted in 1925, and recently redesigned.

72 Ranger's House

A jewel box of desirable objects

One of the most elegant houses in the borough, Ranger's House stands on the western edge of Greenwich Park facing the heath: a well-proportioned redbrick Georgian affair, it was built in 1699 for Admiral Francis Hosier, who famously died of yellow fever while commanding a fleet of ships off the coast of Panama, along with several thousand of his men. The house was inherited by the Earl of Chesterfield and renamed, later becoming the official residence of the Greenwich Park Ranger. Later acquired by English Heritage, its profile was raised in 2002 when it became home to 700 works of art from the collection of Julius Wernher, a wealthy German who made his fortune mining diamonds in South Africa.

It's a beautiful house by any standards, but with the Wernher Collection at its heart, it's a jewel box of desirable objects, sympathetically displayed in generously proportioned rooms with lots of background information. An obsessive collector, Wernher was one of the richest men in Britain when he died, and the treasures here feel like one of Greenwich's unknown pleasures. There are personal devotional items and *memento mori* – seek out a delicate ivory Flemish piece from 1540, which features a rich woman on one side and a skeleton on the other; a stunning collection of jewellery, including a remarkable 17th-century gold ring that displays the Lord's Prayer on a tiny piece of vellum; and an extraordinary gold earring said to be from the 2nd century BC.

There are also valuable paintings, not least 'Madonna of the Pomegranate' by Botticelli, Filipino Lippi's 'Flight out of Egypt', a gorgeous small 'Madonna & Child' by Hans Memling, and English portraits by Romney and Reynolds. There are also many other, later works, most notably scenes from the Dutch Golden Age by painters such as Gerard Dou, Pieter de Hooch and Solomon van Ruisdael.

Address Chesterfield Walk, London, SE10 8QX | Getting there Bus 53 or 386 stop nearby | Hours Apr–Nov, Sun–Thu 11am–5pm; closed the rest of the year | Tip Just a couple of minutes' walk away is Point Hill, a secluded green space from which you can get an excellent view of the central London skyline while enjoying a picnic.

73 Rathmore Hall Benches

Listen to the wall, engage with the benches

The Gaudi-style colourful mosaic benches at the corner of Troughton Road and Rathmore Street look stunning after their recent restoration. In fact they're so fresh following their facelift that nobody would guess their age. Forty years ago, Carol Kenna, Stephen Lobb and Mark Oliver of The Greenwich Mural Workshop were asked to design a mural and benches to liven up the white walls of the Mission Hall Church. This was primarily a collaboration, with the local community as the main driving and creative force.

The beauty of these benches is rooted in their meaning. Local people were forthright in their desire to communicate their message: collectivity and connectivity. Mosaic faces engage with MPs and politicians, with the benches also evoking past and present life in Charlton. The old industries are represented by farming and pottery. The design reminds us that for hundreds of years chalk was dug here, to be burned in lime kilns to make bricks and tiles. Around the corner, the water benches need no introduction, as Father Thames has always loomed large in the borough and with the residents. Shopping is represented too, of course, although in the past this little corner was far from being the shopping zone it is now.

If the power of street art had to be demonstrated, nothing does it more effectively than the mural a few streets away in Floyd Road. Created in 1976 for the local Tenants' Association, this busy work was one of the first murals painted on a London wall. Its primary reason to exist was to stop developers destroying housing and to encourage the council to rehabilitate the properties instead. The mural depicts 'All ages and ethnic backgrounds shown talking, smiling, communicating and working together to fight the people who are happy to destroy their community.' The design is powerful, and the colourful piece seems to have achieved its goal, as 40 years later it remains in place.

Address Corner of Troughton Road and Rathmore Street, London, SE7 7QE; the mural is situated in Floyd Road, SE7 | Getting there Train to Charlton; bus 177 or 180 | Tip There's another stunning mural on Herbert Road in Plumstead, part of a series of works exploring loss and grief by Ant Carver. He drew his inspiration from Rodin's *The Thinker*.

74 The Red House

'More of a poem than a house'

One of south-east London's best kept secrets isn't actually in Green-wich at all, but just a mile or so across the borough border in Bexley: a rare example of early Arts-and-Crafts architecture. Designed and built for William Morris by his friend and architect Philip Webb, and now owned by the National Trust, it nestles among the suburban streets beyond Danson Park. It really was 'all fields around here' when it was built, close to a tiny village outside London known as Hog's Hole, and is the only house in Britain to have been not only lived in by Morris, but designed and built by him too.

Morris moved into Red House in 1860, shortly after marrying the pre-Raphaelite model and muse, Jane Burden. It was commissioned to Morris' specifications – a typically retro-looking structure of eaves and gables, Gothic-style windows and jutting casements with an almost Jacobean look. Meant both as a family home and a venue for meetings of the couple's artistic circle, Morris was also responsible for the interior, and commissioned Edward Burne-Jones – among other pre-Raphaelite artists – to decorate it. Burne-Jones contrib-uted stained glass and wall murals, with various collaborators such as Rossetti and Ford Madox Brown contributing other touches. There's also a wall painting in the main bedroom thought to be by Rosset-ti's wife, Elizabeth Siddall. It was such collaborations that led to the founding of Morris's London design outfit, The Firm, in 1861 – and which ironically led to his eventual return to central London, due to the arduous commute into town.

Outside, the house has a mature garden that would once have been surrounded by countryside. Its shrubs and lawn provide the peace and seclusion of a typically English country garden, and one or two orig-inal fruit trees also survive. Dante Gabriel Rossetti said Red House was 'more of a poem than a house', and he might just have been right.

Address Red House Lane, Bexleyheath, London, DA6 8JF | **Getting there** Bus 89, 422 or 486 to Upton Road | **Hours** Mar–Oct, Wed–Sun 11am–5pm, Nov & Dec, Fri & Sun 11am–4.30pm | **Tip** A short walk from the Red House is Danson Park, a large park with a lovely lake, nature reserve and the 200-year-old 'Charter Oak' – one of the 60 or so 'Great Trees of London'.

75 Richard I

Popular stop-off for locals and tourists alike

First among equals amid a long-established group of pubs tucked away a short distance from the Greenwich tourist track on Royal Hill, Richard I is one of Greenwich's most historic pubs, and also genuinely one of its best – not only for a drink, but also for anyone looking for a bite to eat. It remains more of a local's pub than some of the other establishments in and around the town centre, and is all the better for it. The pub has a long history, too, having served the thirsty folk of West Greenwich since the second half of the 19th century.

The 'Richard' was known affectionately as the 'Tolly' during the 1960s, when it used to serve Tolly Cobbold ales all the way from Ipswich in Suffolk. In those days it was an independently owned, thoroughly working-class watering-hole, but over time it became as gentrified as the rest of West Greenwich, eventually being taken over in the late 1970s by the long-established London brewery Youngs. Spread across two shopfronts, one side used to be an off licence, and this became the public bar, before finally being incorporated with the rest of the pub just over a decade ago.

The pub has since been spruced up and stripped down in line with modern convention. The addition of a glass extension more than doubled the pub's capacity. There's a pleasant garden beyond, which would have been unheard of back when it was a spit-and-sawdust ale house, but even the most ancient regulars would recognise the front of the pub from days gone by. It's still possible to sit within the elegant semi-circles of its bay windows and watch the world go by outside.

On a practical note, the pub serves really good Youngs real ales and craft beers, and also offers decent pub grub all day every day, both in its front bar and the conservatory at the back – and the heaters in the garden mean the outside space can be enjoyed throughout the year. It's a popular stop-off for both in-the-know tourists and locals alike.

Address 52-54 Royal Hill, London, SE10 | **Getting there** Train or DLR to Greenwich; bus 177, 180, 199 or 386 to the bottom of Royal Hill | **Hours** Mon–Sat 11am–11pm, Sun noon–10.30pm | **Tip** Royal Hill is a great place for a pub crawl, starting with the Richard, moving on to the Greenwich Union next door, then the Prince of Greenwich (see ch. 67). After that you could stroll to the Morden Arms at the bottom of Brand Street, before finishing off at the excellent Ashburnham Arms on the other side of Greenwich South. Every one is a great Greenwich local – but remember to drink responsibly!

76 Roman Temple

Greenwich Park's most famous archaeological dig

Formerly known as 'Queen Elizabeth's Bower', you could easily miss one of Greenwich Park's most ancient sites: a low mound not far from the Maze Hill gate on the eastern side of the park, which was first excavated a century ago and thought at the time to be a Roman villa.

Disappointingly, you can't see very much, but – perched high on the hill above the bend in the river far below – it's certainly a good spot to erect a building. This was particularly important in Roman times, when it was close to the route of Watling Street (now the A2), which is believed to have once run right through the park. However, until 20 years ago, no one really knew for sure what the building was. Cue Channel 4's *Time Team*, which visited at the turn of the Millennium and undertook a major investigation, uncovering what's believed to have been a large temple complex. The temple itself occupied the mound alongside a group of associated buildings that would have been situated across what is now a footpath, all surrounded by a low wall. It would have been highly visible by the side of the main Roman road into Londinium, on the highest spot above the city, before it dropped down to cross the Ravensbourne River at Deptford.

The team were amazed to discover objects – lots of coins, plasterwork, roof tiles and a scrap of masonry bearing an inscription to the Emperor and the God Jupiter from a private citizen – that covered the entire period of the Roman occupation of Britain, from the 1st to the 5th century AD. Their finds are now in the collection of the British Museum. Sadly, the excavations were swiftly covered over, so visitors are required to use quite a bit of imagination to reconstruct the scene, which is more or less just a nondescript mound next to the footpath. A nearby information board offers some assistance but in any case the views are as good as any in the park – down over the towers of Canary Wharf and beyond.

Address Greenwich Park, London, SE10 8QY, +44 (0)300 061 2381, www.royalparks.org.uk/parks/greenwich-park | **Getting there** Train to Maze Hill; bus 53 or 54 to Blackheath | **Hours** Always open | **Tip** Walk down the gully just below the temple, cross the path by the fountain and continue through the hollow into the clearing beyond: it's believed that the path across here follows the route of the ancient Roman road into Londinium. Also get a great view of the modern-day London skyline by strolling over to the summit of 'One Tree Hill'.

77 Royal Arsenal

Britain's Arsenal for 300 years

Stretching along the river for over three miles, covering 1,300 acres at its peak in the 18th century, and employing around 100,000 people, there's nothing in London to compare with Woolwich's Royal Arsenal. A place apart from the rest of the town centre, with its own streets, squares, shops, and even transport connections, its elegant Georgian terraces and sought-after river views draw people from all over to enjoy its latest incarnation: 'Royal Arsenal Riverside'.

Known for a time as the 'Woolwich Warren', the Arsenal came about when Henry VIII decided to build a world-beating navy, and established the first naval dockyards in south-east London. He built his mammoth flagship, *Henry Grace à Dieu*, in Woolwich, and added the ordnance factory that grew to be the home of armaments manufacture and storage in Britain for around 300 years.

Open to the public for two decades now, its buildings have been restored as residential accommodation, shops, bars and restaurants. The original gate to the Arsenal still stands on Beresford Square in the centre of Woolwich, but the main entrance is now the other side of the main road. Beyond, Dial Square was the name of the original Woolwich Arsenal FC, which played here before moving to north London in 1910. It's flanked by shops, a couple of restaurants and sporty statues – one representing the football club, the other the goddess Nike, a present from Olympia after the successful 2012 Olympics.

From here you can stroll past the 18th-century brass foundry – until recently used to store overflow artefacts from Greenwich's National Maritime Museum – and the new 'Woolwich Works' district, to the river, where the statues of Peter Burke's *Assembly* sculpture gather in front of two guard rooms. The best thing to do then is just explore: there's plenty of interest, superb river views, and lots of handy pit-stops along the way.

Address London, SE18 6SP | Getting there The Arsenal is due to have its own Crossrail station when the Elizabeth Line finally opens, but until then take the train or DLR to Woolwich Arsenal; bus to Woolwich town centre | Hours Always open | Tip One of our favourite pit-stops while exploring the Arsenal is Boulangerie Jade, a superb local French bakery with branches here and in Blackheath, whose bread and croissants are the best available this side of Paris.

78 Royal Artillery Barracks

Europe's longest building frontage

If there's one building in Greenwich that certainly has the wow factor, it's the Royal Artillery Barracks in Woolwich. Home of the royal artillery from 1776 until just over a decade ago, this was in its day one of the largest military establishments in the world. With the addition of various extensions, at over 300 metres long it also had the longest frontage of any building in Europe, and presents a handsome Georgian spectacle to this day.

The barracks are still partially occupied by the military, but the buildings behind are mainly undistinguished 1950s and 1960s replacements. They're also half empty, as the army is due to move out permanently in 2028. The parade ground at the front is nonetheless a magnificent sight, just crying out for serried ranks of gleaming uniforms and a spot of march-past action. It's difficult to imagine what it might be used for once the army has gone.

You can stroll its length, past a 19th-century memorial to the Crimean War, and from there continue across 'Barrack Field' to The Rotunda. This unique and extremely elegant tent-shaped building was designed in part by John Nash in the early 19th century as a temporary venue for special events and ceremonial occasions – it was the Millennium Dome of its day. Originally standing in central London where it celebrated the return of the Duke of Wellington after his victory over Napoleon, it was relocated to Woolwich in 1818, where it served for many years as the Royal Artillery's dedicated museum. This was moved in 2001, and the Rotunda now serves as a boxing ring for the soldiers of the Kings Troop of the Royal Horse Artillery, whose barracks are located next door. The horses and soldiers of the Kings Troop are mobilised on ceremonial occasions (for which you may see them practising on the common); there's space for up to 140 horses, outdoor and indoor riding schools, as well as a vet, saddler, tailor and blacksmith.

Address Repository Road, London, SE18 4BH | **Getting there** Train or DLR to Woolwich Arsenal; multiple buses pass the far side of the barracks on their way to Woolwich town centre, including 53, 54 or 422; alternatively, take bus 89 to nearby Shooter's Hill | **Hours** Always open | **Tip** Hang around Blackheath any morning and you might be lucky enough to see the horses of the Kings Troop making their way to central London on a regular exercise ride – an impressive sight, with around 30 horses managed by just a dozen or so riders.

79 Royal Blackheath Golf Club

Historical club and elegant Eltham Lodge

When Queen Elizabeth I died in 1603, James VI of Scotland moved his court to Greenwich, arriving with many courtiers and officers along with their retinue. In those days, not many English folks had seen a golf club, let alone played the sport. Imagine their bewilderment when they came across groups of Scots hitting balls with sticks on the heath! As early as 1608, the golfers had settled for a piece of land which was going to be home to the Royal Blackheath Golf Club. This made it, in effect, the first golf club in England, although it claims to be Scottish by birth.

The association with royalty didn't stop then. In 1660, King Charles II signed the deeds of the Tudor manors in Eltham to John Shaw, a financier and first Baronet, permitting him to build a new lodge there. Hugh May, who had worked on Windsor Castle, designed The Lodge, which is now a splendid clubhouse. The deeds with Charles II's signature have pride of place in the club museum, along with 400 years' worth of trophies, medals and Captains' goblets. Also notice as you go upstairs that there is no landing at any point – a unique feature. As well as providing golfers with a historical club, the clubhouse opens for afternoon teas, and the Eagleton Gray room is a spectacular setting for special occasions. The original plasterwork on the ceiling still baffles many professionals with its intricacy, and the paintings on the red walls don't disappoint either. See if you can spot Terence Cuneo's trademark little mouse on the Captain's table oil painting.

Golfing is one of the most popular sports in the UK, the club is as strong today as it has ever been. Men and women of all abilities are welcomed. For golfers looking for something a little different, the 17th hole with its unique design, is a challenging but enjoyable feature.

Address Court Road, London, SE9 5AF, +44 (0)20 8850 1795, www.royalblackheath.com | **Getting there** Train to Mottingham or Eltham; various buses | **Hours** See website for current information on visiting; look into joining a guided tour of the Clubhouse too | **Tip** Need a little practice? Head for Greenwich Peninsula Golf Range (265 Tunnel Avenue, London, SE10 0QE) – a riverside golf driving range with 60 bays, and a mini 18-hole adventure course.

80 Royal Observatory

The beginning of time and the top of the world

Built in 1676, the Royal Observatory was the official home and workplace of the 'Astronomer Royal' – a post created by Charles II to perfect the art of navigation, which was crucial to British exploration and power. It's an amazing collection of buildings in a location selected by architect Christopher Wren for its elevated position, close to London, yet far enough away to enjoy clear skies.

Like so much in Greenwich, money was always an issue, so the building was constructed using ships' timbers and salvage from the Tower of London, and its first incumbent, John Flamsteed, was expected to live on just £100 a year (about £12,000 now), including all expenses and equipment. Later Astronomers Royal included Edmund Halley, who discovered the famous comet (see ch. 90), and James Bradley, who between 1736 and 1759 presided over John Harrison's solving of the longitude problem with his famous clocks (H1-H4), which are displayed on the main exhibition floor. The real treat, however, is the Octagon Room, with its picture windows and ornate ceiling. It must have been a lonely life, high up above the trees and buildings, and both here and in the private apartments, it's easy to conjure the ghosts of astronomers, gazing at the heavens and taking measurements.

In the courtyard you can stand on the Prime Meridian, which marks zero degrees longitude, and see an exhibition explaining how the meridian has moved over the years – mostly due to astronomers' whims – along with the transit rooms of the various astronomers, and their equipment. Climb the stairs above the souvenir shop up for a look at the Great Equatorial Telescope – one of the largest in the world when it was introduced in 1893, and impressive even today. While the observatory now has a purely historical function, its scientific role having moved to Herstmonceux in 1958, it's a striking monument to Britain's central role in the world of science.

Address Greenwich Park, London, +44(0)20 8312 6608 | Getting there Train to Greenwich or Maze Hill; DLR to Cutty Sark; buses 129, 177, 180, 188, 199, 286 or 386 to Greenwich town centre | Hours Wed–Sun 10am–4pm | Tip If possible, coincide your visit with the falling of the red time ball on the tower of Flamsteed House. Just before 1pm each day the ball rises to the top of the mast, and falls at exactly 1pm – a signal used to confirm the precise time to seafarers on the river since 1833.

81 Rustic Fountain

Known to Pagan worshippers as Motherstone Fountain

Greenwich Park is many things to many people but its historical importance means that among other things it's a place of pilgrimage for
Pagan worshippers. One of their gathering places is Rustic Fountain,
also known as The Motherstone Fountain, situated on Lovers Walk.

This public fountain was built in the 1860s and recently restored.
The drinking hole drew water from a nearby spring, and in its func-
tioning days, two metal cups were chained to the bowl. However, in
the mid-1950s, concerns were raised regarding the safety of the Victorian lead piping, and as a result the spring was capped, making the
fountain redundant. But still, water fills the bowl!

The park has several other fountains: an ornamental pink granite
feature dating from 1894, a sculptural affair in the Herb Garden, three
utilitarian bubblers funded by Tiffany and Co, plus a few others. So
what's the attraction of the Rustic Fountain? Firstly, it has a striking
design, with a scallop-shaped bowl, and perfect arch carved within the
blue-tinged stones. The Preseli bluestone stones appear to date from
much earlier than the 1800s, and are believed to originate from the
Bluebell Hill stone circle in Kent, itself connected with Stonehenge.
Indeed, the fountain does resemble a Neolithic monument.

The fountain is sometimes adorned by offerings such as flowers,
crystals, wands and candles left by worshippers. Local pagans still
commune here with the unbridled goddess Lilith and the Greek
Hecate, an early incarnation of the triple goddess Diana. The latter
is a deity familiar to the park, as evidence of a Romano-Celtic temple, possibly dedicated to the hunting goddess, was discovered nearby
during the making of archaeological TV programme *Time Team* (see
ch. 76). Other signs of worship are evident throughout the park: on
excavating burial mounds, archaeologists have unearthed swords,
shields, and other artefacts dating back to the seventh century.

Address Lovers Walk, London, SE10 8XJ | **Getting there** Best approach from Vanbrugh gate; once in the park, follow the signs for Queen Elizabeth's Oak | **Hours** Daily 6am – 6pm (hours vary by season) | **Tip** If you think Lovers Walk is an unusual name for a public highway, it's not the only one in the borough: Kings Butts in Eltham, Ha-Ha Road near Shooter's Hill, and Pigsty Alley in Greenwich are just a few others.

82 Sayes Court Park
Round the mulberry bush with an environmentalist

Deptford's Evelyn Ward is steeped in history. Drake, Raleigh and Cook all embarked upon their voyages from the docks near the contemporary Sayes Court Park, and John Evelyn, a 17th-century polymath, lived in Sayes Court. Evelyn was born into a land-owning family, and while he is mainly remembered for his diaries, he was also a scholar, a founder member of the Royal Society, and a horticulturist. He also introduced salad to the English diet!

Evelyn left us an important legacy, with his writings about trees and air quality still resonating today. Several of the streets surrounding the park are named after him. The writer cherished his garden. The formal oval design surrounded by a 400-foot-long holly hedge was his pride and joy. Sadly, this was badly damaged in an incident involving a drunken Peter the Great and a wheelbarrow (see ch. 62).

In 1729, the house was demolished, and his garden is now buried beneath a housing estate. In the 1870s, pioneer thinker and social reformer Octavia Hill led a campaign to preserve the grounds, but to her disappointment this was unsuccessful. By then, the government had sold much of the site back to Evelyn's descendants, and together with Hill they created Sayes Court Park – a recreation ground for use by local people. Hill went on to co-found the National Trust.

The public park, located on the Thames Path, still carries Evelyn's legacy. The Evelyn 200 project aims to plant 200 trees to highlight the poor air quality in the ward, and improve the urban environment. Several have already been planted, including a Turkish hazelnut tree. Samples of the ancient mulberry tree that faces one of the entrances have been analysed, and although it's difficult to date exactly, the results indicate a hybrid tree that's 200 to 300 years old. This means the story of Peter, future Tsar, planting it as a sorry gesture, is probably little more than a legend.

Address London, SE8 3BD, with access via Sayes Court Street or Grove Street | **Getting there** Train or DLR to Surrey Quays, then bus 188 or 199; train to Deptford then bus or walk; bus 47, 188 or 199 | **Tip** Twinkle Park, situated near Sayes Court Park, is an unusual park with a large pond, wildlife gardens, gazebo and a mosaic floor compass made by Greenwich Mural Workshop. The park was designed in association with local residents.

83 Severndroog Castle

A people's castle with spectacular views

On Shooter's Hill, at the highest point between London and Paris, stands a folly with breathtaking views across seven counties. Its name is the anglicised version of Suvarnadurg, a fort located on a small Indian island in the Arabian sea, between Mumbai and Goa. The fortress was a strategic point for maritime trade. In 1755, the Peshwas and the British joined forces, under the command of Commodore William James, to launch an attack on Suvarnadurg, the Golden Fort – also known as the 'Pirate Stronghold'.

Thanks to his maritime victory, James returned to England a very wealthy man. He opted to live in fashionable Soho, and acquired a country estate in Eltham. After his death, his wife had a memorial built to celebrate their love and his military victory. She called it the Severndroog Castle. Lady James was a person with expensive tastes. This is reflected in the decoration, gilded ceilings, chandeliers, tall windows with pointed arches, and the surrounding wooded moat. In those days, follies were very popular, and the Severndroog quickly became a tourist attraction. Since then, the place has known many reversals of fortune. It was marked for demolition on many occasions.

At the beginning of the 21st century, after years of neglect, a campaign group led by determined local people stopped its sale to private developers. They then restored the place to its former glory. Eleven years later the scaffolding and fences came down, and the historic building was ready to welcome the public once more.

On the ground floor, there's a charming café offering delicious homemade cakes, a treat after a walk in Oxleas Woodlands (see ch. 57), or after enjoying a guided visit and climbing the 97 stairs to the viewing platform. Aside from the views, Severndroog is a place for people to enjoy seasonal events, evening concerts, family days and weddings. The folly has become a people's castle.

Address Castle Wood, London, SE18 3RT, www.severndroogcastle.org.uk | Getting there
Train to Eltham or Falconwood, both a couple of miles away; bus 89, 244 or 486 to Memorial
Hospital on Shooter's Hill | Hours Can be seen all year round, but to go inside visit Mar–Oct,
Thu, Fri & Sun 12.30–4.30pm, Nov–Mar, Thu, Fri & Sun 11am–3pm; tickets for the viewing
platform: adults £3, children £2.50, families £8 | Tip Less than a mile away across the
A207/Shooter's Hill at 51 Brinklow Crescent, London, SE18 3HG, you'll find Shrewsbury
Tumulus – a 75-foot-diameter burial mound dating back to the Bronze Age.

84 Sewell Memorial Plaque

A war hero immortalised in stone

On 29 August, 1918, Lieutenant Cecil Sewell was just 23 years old when he gave his life to save his comrades. The armistice was signed just over a month later. His story is incredibly moving. Born in Royal Hill, Greenwich, in 1895, and one of nine children, his five brothers and father enlisted. Before 1914, Cecil was studying law, in the family tradition. Indeed, his brother Herbert was a barrister. But the war was going to change all that. As well as Cecil, three other Sewell brothers would not return. Cecil's actions on the Western Front were so heroic that he was posthumously honoured with the Victoria Cross, the highest and most prestigious British military award. His parents received his Victoria Cross medal from the hands of King George V at the end of 1918. His citation tells the story of a man brave beyond his years.

On the fatal day at Fremincourt, he was in command of a section of Whippet Light Tanks, when one of the vehicles slipped into a large shell-hole. Lieutenant Sewell got out of his own tank, 'Caesar II', to rescue the crew of another Whippet. He promptly ran across the open ground under enemy fire. When he reached the stricken vehicle, the tank door was jammed against the shell-hole. Digging away the entrance, he released the door, saving all the men inside. That's when he spotted one of his own crew injured behind Caesar II, and yet again, he heroically crossed the ground to his assistance. While dressing the wounds of the badly injured driver, Cecil was fatally hit in the stomach. When they recovered his body, his arms were wrapped protectively around his crew-mate.

In August 2013, the government announced a campaign to honour Victoria Cross recipients from World War I in the form of commemorative paving stones. The Borough of Greenwich has four such paving-plaques, and Cecil Sewell is the youngest of the brave men immortalised in stone here.

Address The VC stone memorial to Lieutenant Sewell is located at the junction of Crooms Hill and Gloucester Circus, London, SE10 8RX | Getting there Train to Greenwich; bus 177, 180, 199 or 386 to Royal Hill, then a two-minute walk up the hill – the Circus is on the left | Tip Due to its strong military connections, Greenwich Borough abounds with memorials. On the corner of Charlton Way and Maze Hill, there's a large stone wall commemorating 1,800 lives lost in both World Wars. Its peculiarity is that rather than have the names on the memorial, the Roll of Honour was placed inside the monument.

85 Sir Walter Raleigh

The Queen's favourite polymath lays down his cloak

Elizabeth I was born in the royal palace at Greenwich, and this was her favourite residence throughout her reign – a place not only of happy childhood memories, but also a perfect place for the warrior queen to keep an eye on her navy. It's perhaps fitting, then, that the statue of one of her favourite courtiers, Sir Walter Raleigh, stands on the same site in what is now the Royal Naval College, in front of the museum and information centre at Pepys House. He cuts a suitably dashing figure in doublet and hose, for it was in this locality that the knight, adventurer, poet and polymath apocryphally laid down his cloak over a puddle to keep the monarch's shoes dry.

Raleigh was an entitled sort of fellow, who thought nothing of setting off for the Americas to found a colony or two. Today, he's best known for bringing back potatoes and tobacco from the New World. As one of the Queen's favourites, he was knighted in 1585, and given various estates in Ireland. He blotted his copybook in 1592, however, by bedding and then secretly marrying one of the Elizabeth's maids, landing himself in the Tower as a result.

On his release, Raleigh undertook further voyages to Spain and the Azores, and later on an expedition to find the fabled golden city of El Dorado in South America. Here his son was killed, and Raleigh almost started a fresh war with Spain. Perhaps as a result of this, he fell out of favour with the queen's successor, James I, who again imprisoned him in the Tower, this time for over a decade.

Raleigh was by now used to the rollercoaster life of a high-flying courtier, and accepted his fate graciously, spending his time in prison writing the five-volume *History of the World*, and adding to his many poems, before being beheaded for treason in 1618. Aware of his reputation to the last, his final words were apparently, 'I would not have my enemies think I quaked from fear. Strike Man, Strike!'.

Address Cutty Sark Gardens, London, SE10 9LW | **Getting there** Train to Greenwich or Maze Hill; DLR to Cutty Sark; buses 129, 177, 180, 188, 199, 286 or 386 to Greenwich town centre | **Hours** Always open | **Tip** There's a memorial to another explorer a few steps away on the riverside walk – a granite obelisk that commemorates Lieutenant Bellot (1826–1852), a young French naval officer, who died heroically while trying to rescue survivors of the ill-fated Franklin Arctic expedition.

86 Skittle Alley
Rum and skittles

One of the lesser-known features of the former Royal Naval College – and viewable only if taking a guided tour from Pepys House – is the complex's Victorian Skittle Alley, sitting snugly beneath the somewhat better-known Naval College Chapel. Constructed in 1864, it was created for the benefit of the Greenwich pensioners, who the authorities were keen to discourage from spending all their time drinking and gambling. A library had been added in 1824, but most sailors were not great readers so it was felt that some sort of active pursuit would be best – hence the skittle alley.

Until the late 18th century the cellars here were occupied by the Naval College's operating theatre. It was an ideal location for this purpose: this was before the invention of anaesthesia, and no one could hear the screams of the amputees and other unfortunates who came under the surgeon's knife. It's a gruesome thought, and you might prefer to concentrate on the skittles, but before you do, take a look at the window sills: these have deep grooves dating back to the time when they were used by surgeons to sharpen their blades.

As usual, the college made very little money available for construction of the skittle alley, which meant much of it was put together by the pensioners themselves using whatever materials they could find. Like so much in Greenwich, a lot of the wood was rescued from the wrecks of old sailing ships, and the balls themselves are re-purposed practice cannon balls; keen bowlers will be disappointed to learn that they're extremely heavy, with no holes to provide grip.

The alley itself is a two-lane affair, with a channel in the middle along which the balls miraculously travel back to the bowler. Players have to put the skittles back up themselves, however, or have someone willing to do it for them. If you'd like to have a go yourself, the skittle alley is occasionally accessible on open days and special occasions.

Address Old Royal Naval College, London, SE10 9NN | Getting there Train to Greenwich or Maze Hill; DLR to Cutty Sark; buses 129, 177, 180, 188, 199, 286 or 386 to Greenwich town centre | Hours Daily 10am–5pm | Tip The remains of a sporting arena of a different kind were recently discovered across the road in front of the Queen's House – Henry VIII's jousting or 'tilt' yard. There's nothing to see, but it's indicative of the collision of different eras in the Greenwich World Heritage site.

87 St Alfege Church

Invaders created a martyr, Hawksmoor a masterpiece

A monumental structure amid the bustle of central Greenwich, there's been a church on this site since the 11th century – built as a shrine to the little-known St Alfege, martyred here in 1012. Alfege was Archbishop of Canterbury at the time, and was taken hostage by the Danes, who invaded England in 1010. After he refused to be traded for a ransom, they killed the saint in traditional Viking fashion: by thrashing him to death with ox-bones. After his death, he became one of the most venerated saints in the country, with a shrine at Canterbury. A stone near the altar commemorating St Alfege reads: *He who dies for justice, dies for Christ.* Eventually his remains were moved to London, and the church at Greenwich became a prestigious and holy place, with Henry VIII believed to have been baptised here.

Nowadays the church is perhaps better known for other historical figures, many of whom are buried here. These include the British naval hero James Wolfe, who lived in Greenwich and won a memorable battle at Quebec in 1759; Sir John Julius Angerstein, one of the founders of Lloyds of London, known for the art collection that formed the foundation of the National Gallery; Samuel Enderby, whose Enderby Wharf dispatched whaling ships all over the world in the late 18th century, and who gets a mention in Herman Melville's *Moby-Dick;* and Thomas Tallis – one of Tudor England's great composers, and the church organist for over 40 years.

The church's roof collapsed in the late 17th century, and was completely rebuilt between 1712 and 1714, in the contemporary style of Nicholas Hawksmoor – perhaps the most famous pupil of Christopher Wren and John Vanbrugh. Hawksmoor's monumental design was inspired by both the Baroque extravagances of the time and the ancient temples of Rome and Greece. The result? A uniquely harmonious interior that is simultaneously intimate and grand.

Address Greenwich Church Street, London, SE10 9BJ, www.st-alfege.org.uk | Getting there Train to Greenwich or Maze Hill; DLR to Cutty Sark; bus 129, 177, 180, 188, 199, 286 or 386 to Greenwich town centre | Hours Mon–Fri 11am–4pm, Sat 10am–4pm, Sun noon–4pm | Tip After seeing the church, admire the mini terrace of Georgian houses on St Alfege Passage, and stroll through to the pocket-sized park behind, where scattered gravestones reveal its original function as St Alfege's churchyard.

88 Standards of Length

Ensure the accuracy of your measuring stick

Nowadays, only three countries in the world still officially use the Imperial System of Measurements: the USA, Liberia and Myanmar. The UK adopted metric units in 1965, but continues to work with both systems: Brits still measure long distances in miles, but are likely to weigh food in grammes. This mixed use often baffles visitors, and exact measurements were for years a common bone of contention, and as early as 1668 there were calls for standardisation.

A set of standard lengths was first introduced at the Houses of Parliament in the 1760s. While these were destroyed by fire in 1834, the problem was resolved with the Weights and Measures Act of 1824, which redefined common units of measurement in England. That wasn't the end of the matter, however. In 1838, the seventh Astronomer Royal, George Biddell Airy, was asked to chair a committee to reinstate the new national standards in weights and measures. Airy was an influential advisor to the government, and an authority: in the 19th century the post of Astronomer Royal was the highest office in Civil Science. With so much confusion, industry and the public needed a solid foundation to work from.

A plaque showing British Imperial Standards of Length produced by the scientific instrument makers Troughton and Simms was mounted outside the observatory gates in January 1859. The plaque shows one British yard, two feet, one foot, six inches, and three inches. The Public Standards of Length plaque served two purposes: it had a very important public relations purpose, being a visible sign of the observatory's role in moderating national scientific and technical standards, and it gave exact measurements. In these days, the Royal Observatory was eager to demonstrate the practical usefulness of their work and the public of the time used it to check the accuracy of their rulers, and so can you.

Address The observatory is located in Greenwich Park, Blackheath Avenue, London, SE10 8XJ | **Getting there** Car parking is available for visitors with disabilities only – limited pre-booked spaces are available via bookings@rmg.co.uk; the Royal Observatory is at the top of a fairly steep hill; allow 15 minutes on foot from King William Walk; DLR or boat to Cutty Sark; train to Maze Hill or Blackheath, then a 20-minute flat walk across the heath | **Hours** See website for current information on visiting | **Tip** Next to the Standards of Length is the Shepherd master clock – the first clock to show Greenwich Mean Time – GMT – directly to the public.

The Shepherd 24-hour Gate Clock

This is one of the earliest electrically driven public clocks and was installed here in 1852. The dial always shows Greenwich Mean Time (GMT). In summer Britain converts to British Summer Time (BST), which is an hour ahead of GMT, and the clock then appears one hour "slow".

Being a 24-hour clock, the hour hand marks noon (XII) at the bottom of the dial and midnight (0) at the top. The time shown is accurate to 0.5 of a second.

The Time Ball

The red time ball on top of Flamsteed House is one of the world's first visual time signals. It was installed in 1833 though the present one dates to 1919 to enable navigators on ships in the Thames to check their marine chronometers.

The Time Ball drops daily at 1300hrs GMT in winter, BST in summer). It is raised halfway up the mast at 1255hrs as a preparatory signal and to the top 2 minutes before it drops.

HEIGHT ABOVE
MEAN SEA LEVEL
AT NEWLYN
151·70 FEET.

Ordnance Survey Bench Mark

The small plate marked 'G 1690') is an Ordnance Survey bench mark. Similar marks appear on walls and buildings across the country. The height of each above sea level has been measured and recorded. Dating from the 1940s, this particular mark is a replacement for an older mark that once existed nearby.

Public Standards of Length

These British Imperial Standards were first mounted outside the Observatory main gates some time before 1866, to enable the public to check measures of length.

This stated length is the distance between the inner faces of the two D-shaped studs.

BRITISH YARD

TWO FEET

ONE FOOT   SIX INCHES   THREE INCHES

89 _ St George's Church

Woolwich's most evocative ruin

Across the main road from the wide sweep of the Royal Artillery Barracks, it's easy to miss St George's Garrison Church. But this wasn't always the case. Pictures show that this was a substantial structure when it was built in 1862 – elegantly proportioned, decorative and solid. But it was virtually destroyed by a bomb in 1944 and never recovered, so what you see now is more or less a ruin, topped at one end with a canopy so it can still be used for outdoor services.

The church was commissioned by Lord Herbert (a man referenced locally in the former military hospital on Shooters Hill Road, as well in a nearby pub and the road on which it's located), Secretary of State for War during the Crimean War, who was charged with improving the physical and spiritual lot of the common infantryman following the terrible tales of Florence Nightingale from the Front. Designed by the highly prolific Victorian architect Thomas Henry Wyatt, it was an important landmark in its day, and nowadays provides an enduring and rather moving memorial to the fallen of the artillery through every war Britain has fought since the Crimean, including the recent conflicts in Iraq and Afghanistan.

There's not much left of the interior, but what does remain is worth noting, specifically the St George & Dragon mosaic above the altar, and the lists which record gunners who have received the Victoria Cross, right up to the present day. There's also a small plaque on the south wall which remembers the rest, including Fusilier Lee Rigby, who was killed just around the corner from here in 2013, aged just 25. Have a look, too, at the other fragments of mosaics, including the peacock and the phoenix on either side of the altar. Looking at these, along with the pulpit and still partially mosaicked arches, visitors come away with a real sense of loss – not just for the men who died, but also for the church itself.

Address Grand Depot Road, London, SE18 6XJ, www.stgeorgeswoolwich.org | Getting there DLR or train to Woolwich Arsenal; various buses to Woolwich town centre | Hours Apr–Sep, Sun 10.15am–4pm, Oct–Mar, Sun 10.15am–1pm | Tip Wander down into central Woolwich or up to The Bull pub on Shooter's Hill to try south-east London's best and most authentic Neapolitan pizzas at Rust Bucket Pizza – or order a delivery at www.rustbucketpizzaco.co.uk.

90 St Margaret's Church

The Westminster of Lee

There's no denying that Lee is not in the Royal Borough of Greenwich, but Lewisham. However, St Margaret's Church shouldn't be missed, due to its relevance to the history of Greenwich. The Old Churchyard, only 30 minutes' walk from the Royal Observatory, is the last resting place of no less than three Astronomers Royal. The most famous of this trio is Edmond Halley, second Astronomer Royal, best known for calculating the orbit of the comet that was later named after him. He shares his resting place with John Pond, who was regarded as the best positional astronomer of his generation, while Nathaniel Bliss is buried in an unmarked grave.

The church interior's sheer beauty is reason enough to visit. It's one of the best-preserved and restored examples of Gothic revivalist architecture in London. Some of the best late-19th-century craftspeople were employed under the direction of James Brook. Inspired by the pre-Raphaelite era, the stained-glass windows were created by the famous firm of Clayton and Bell, who also worked on King's College, Cambridge. The east end stained-glass window, with its gathering of angels, almost shines in natural daylight. Specialist painting techniques such as marouflage were applied to the walls and look like frescos. The High Altar was beautifully carved by Violet Pinwill, a remarkable professional woodcarver. Its dark patina shows off the skilful carvings, and enhances the church's vivid colours.

This church has a very long history. The first reference to a place of worship dedicated to St Margaret of Antioch dates back to around 1120. The saint was very popular in medieval times, and was a favourite of Edward the Confessor and the crusaders – although this could be considered a slightly incongruous choice, as Margaret is the patron of expectant mothers and difficult births! Amazingly, the early church tower dating back to 1275 still stands in the Old Churchyard.

Address Lee Terrace, London, SE13 5DL; the Visitors' Centre is on Brandram Road, London, SE13 5EA, +44 (0)20 8318 9643, office@stmargaretslee.org.uk | Getting there Bus 54, 89 and 108 to St Margaret's Church/Brandram Road; train (Blackheath or Lewisham mainline) and DLR stations, then bus 89 and 108 | Hours Open for worship; the church is open for visits on the first Saturday of the month 10.30am–4.30pm | Tip Halley's meridian line of 1725, prior to the Prime Meridian, can be seen both inside and outside the Royal Observatory in Greenwich; look for the marker on the wall and/or the lectern with explanations.

91 St Nicholas Church

Resting place of Deptford's most famous murder victim

The tower is the giveaway at this Deptford church, a rough-hewn buttressed affair that is in fact the only remnant of an originally medieval structure. The upper part of the tower was destroyed during a gale in 1901, but the flint and stone bottom half dates back to the foundation of the church in the 12th century.

The remainder of the church is a brick neo-classical structure, built in the late 17th century, when the churchyard's notorious skull and crossbones sculptures were added to either side of the gate. This was not, as used to be believed, to denote the presence of pirates, but simply an indicator of the charnel house within. A century or so earlier, on 30 May, 1593, the Elizabethan playwright and putative spy Christopher Marlowe was killed in Deptford at the age of just 29, and his passing is marked by a simple memorial against the wall of the old churchyard, close to his unmarked grave.

Marlowe was a handsome, daredevil sort of chap who was allegedly recruited as a spy while at Cambridge. He is believed to have been a homosexual and an atheist, and in the pay of Elizabeth I's favourite spymaster, Francis Walsingham, who famously brought down Mary, Queen of Scots. It was once thought that Marlowe had been stabbed during a drunken brawl, but it now seems more likely that he was formally executed for fear he might incriminate others.

Unfortunately, the church is kept locked except for services. If you can get inside, the reward is another memorial to Marlowe, and an altarpiece decorated with spectacular wooden carvings of the Prophet Isaiah and St John by the prolific 17th-century craftsman Grinling Gibbons. There's also a wonderful older pulpit supported by the carved figure of a small boy. Overall, the church is a peaceful and relatively unknown spot, a real remnant of medieval Deptford – a world away from the well-travelled artery of nearby Creek Road.

Address Deptford Green, London, SE8 3DQ, +44 (0)20 8692 2749, www.stnicholaschurchdeptford.org | Getting there Train to Deptford; various buses to Creek Road | Hours Open for services only | Tip The church is tucked away at the top of so-called Deptford Green, on a cut-through to the river path and pocket-sized Twinkle Park. From here you can follow the high wall of the Master Shipwright's House to a small beach that's exposed at low tide, or stroll through the green space of Charlotte Turner Gardens to the excellent Dog and Bell pub (see ch. 20) – little known by anyone other than the locals, and all the better for it!

92 St Paul's Church
Rome's Baroque glories – in Deptford!

The spire of St Paul's Church, just off Deptford's famous high street, rises above the grand, colonnaded, semi-circular portico of this historic landmark. Designed by Thomas Archer and opened in 1730, the church was built during the reign of Queen Anne as part of a scheme to construct up to 50 new churches in the further-flung suburbs of London. It represented a spectacular attempt to recreate the Counter-Reformation in London, with a curving entrance that was rather fancifully modelled on the more diminutive structure of Santa Maria delle Pace, situated just off Piazza Navona in Rome.

If you're able to gain entrance to the church, it's possible to enjoy the almost perfectly symmetrical and very large interior, with huge Corinthian columns and an incredibly ornate plaster ceiling. Both of these features echo another Roman church: Sant' Agnese in Agone, by the Italian Baroque architect Francesco Borromini, which Archer would have seen on his Grand Tour in the 1680s. Otherwise, just stroll around and observe the various funerary monuments which indicate the historic importance of this church – and, perhaps, how things have changed in the surrounding neighborhood. Fortunately, the building presents a rather elegant and unexpected sight amid Deptford's otherwise solidly urban landscape, squeezed between the high street and the busy dual carriageway beyond. If you can't access the church, content yourself with a stroll around the churchyard, which is usually open from morning until early evening every day.

Could there be a more unexpected place for one of London's most Baroque, Roman-style buildings? Probably not. But there is no single building that better encapsulates the history of this remarkable – and remarkably changed – part of the city. Deptford has always been a neighbourhood of sharp contrasts, and this church remains one of the greatest and most eye-catching historic landmarks.

Address Mary Ann Gardens, London, SE8 3DP, +44 (0)20 8692 7449 | Getting there Train to Deptford; DLR to Deptford Bridge | Hours Closed except for services | Tip Across the main road from the church, the Crossfields Estate was once home to Mark Knopfler and his brother David, the founder members of Dire Straits, who played their first-ever gig in 1977 at an impromptu summer festival held on the patch of grass outside. A plaque on the side of Farrer House marks the occasion.

93 Suffragettes Walk

No plaque, no statue for local key figures

Many of the key figures in the Women's Right to Vote movement lived and worked in Greenwich borough but despite the strength and number of its local membership, there's very little to commemorate this important period, so we have put together a short walk to trace this close-knit and transformational group of women, whose activities changed the face of society.

This starts with Edith New's abode at 68 Royal Hill, situated in central Greenwich but with no plaque to acknowledge her residence – just a charming, private three-storey house with a heart embedded in the dormer window. The National Union of Women's Suffrage operated as a local branch from this location and Edith was one of the first suffragettes to use vandalism as a tactic, smashing two windows at 10 Downing Street, for which she was sentenced to two months in Holloway prison. She continued her protest with a hunger strike.

This strategy was also used by Emily Wilding Davison, who was force-fed on 49 occasions. She's most remembered for her final protest, when she jumped in front of King George V's horse at Epsom racecourse in 1913, resulting in her death. Born just 39 years earlier, in Roxburgh House on Vanbrugh Park Road West, her loss must have been a bitter blow for the local suffragettes, who included Millicent Fawcett, educated in Blackheath and president of the largest suffrage society of its time. By far the most photographed suffragette was Rosa May Billinghurst, also known as the 'cripple suffragette'. She formed the Greenwich branch of the Women's Social and Political Union, based at 7 Oakcroft Road, now in Lewisham, just off Blackheath. Rosa May attended demonstrations and suffered police brutality.

The Suffragettes may not be officially acknowledged in the area, but we can follow in their footsteps, and end our walk on Blackheath, where they flew kites for relaxation.

Getting there From Royal Hill, walk towards Point Hill, follow the street all the way, and it turns into a path leading you to Blackheath Hill; the heath is on your left; continue straight for a kilometre to Oakcroft Road | Tip Royal Hill is a charming area with quaint food shops and a coffee place to meet friends for a healthy bite and a chat: Royal Teas offers homemade and vegan foods (76 Royal Hill, www.royalteascafe.co.uk).

94 Tarn Park Bird Sanctuary
Avian tranquillity amid the hubbub

To understand how this small hidden park managed to survive in the midst of a busy concrete jungle, we have to cast our minds back to the days when the Tarn was known as Starbucks Pond. Then, Eltham Palace was a royal retreat and the birthplace of Edward II. The estate was majestic. At some point, the grounds incorporated three lakes. Tarn Park is just a fragment left from the royal grounds, much neglected until 1935, when it was purchased by the Council for a public park.

The ornamental lake is fed by Little Quaggy, a small local stream, via a concrete channel situated at the back of the park. However there is a bit of a puzzle here, the wild meadow pound, next to the Tarn, doesn't seem to have any source of water, and is a bit of a mystery. A possible explanation is that the water could originate from the 18th-century ice well. The latter is one of the earliest of its kind, and was used by kitchen staff at Eltham Palace.

Tarn Park is one of the very few bird sanctuaries in the capital. It's home to a wide variety of wildlife: Canada geese and many types of ducks totter around to the delight of small children, and there are blackbirds, jays, tits, woodpeckers and herons among the species fluttering around this little oasis. A terrapin or two and a few goldfish have also found their way to the Tarn.

Sadly, and despite all the efforts of volunteers, the Tarn is overgrown with duckweed, and the water is very green. Friends of the Tarn is a group instrumental in its preservation, and it's thanks to them that joggers, nature-lovers and generations of families are able to enjoy the area, and its abundant fauna. The Friends created a Nature and Butterfly garden, and have lovingly restored bird nesting boxes with funds collected at special events such as tea-parties. There is also a picnic area for visitors who want to spend a little more time here – just don't forget your bird-watching binoculars.

Address The Tarn, Court Road, London, SE9 5AQ, www.thetarn.org | Getting there
Train to Mottingham with direct trains to London Bridge, Waterloo East, Charing Cross
and Cannon Street on the Sidcup line; bus 124, 126 or 161; on foot, The Green Chain
Walk, south east London's walking route linking 300 open spaces by 50 miles of footpaths,
passes through the Tarn | Hours Daily 9am – dusk | Tip The Tarn is adjacent to the UK's
oldest golf club: the Royal Blackheath Golf Club (see ch. 79).

95 Thames Barrier
Protecting London from the sea

Not dissimilar to a great urban sculpture, the 10 gates of the Thames Barrier span half a kilometre across the river from the London Borough of Greenwich to Newham. Opened in 1982, it's the second-largest movable flood defence in the world, designed to protect London from flooding as a result of changes in the tide. Needless to say, it's done a good job considering the capital's long history of floods. The worst of these was the Great Flood of 1928, which saw 14 people killed, thousands made homeless, and a considerable area of the city centre flooded when the Thames and Chelsea Embankment collapsed. Nowadays, thanks to the effectiveness of the barrier, we could almost believe that the tidal section of the Thames has been tamed. Recent facts and figures are worrying, however: while in the 1980s there were just four closures, since then it has been shut a total of 193 times.

The only safe way to see the barrier working is to attend the annual testing day, when visitors can observe the mechanism in action from the riverfront. This is an impressive spectacle throughout, but when the gates are raised to 90 degrees to put the barrier in 'defence' position, a 'white rush' effect takes place, stirring up the riverbed, and that moment is something to see. The barrier has no individual trigger level for closure. The closing process is guided by a mathematical matrix, and the decision is made by the Thames Barrier Duty Controller. If you've missed the testing day, the next best thing is to watch the virtual technical tour film and the interactive displays in the friendly and informative Information Centre.

Since the Thames has been managed more carefully, it is the cleanest it has been for 150 years. Nowdays, seals and their pups, dolphins and porpoises have all repopulated the river. It's not unusual to see whole families of marine animals frolicking between the Thames Barrier and Greenwich.

Address Eastmoor Street, London, SE7 8LX, +44 (0)20 8305 4188, www.gov.uk/the-thames-barrier | Getting there Spot the Thames Barrier from the river on a boat tour; train to Charlton on Woolwich Road, then a mile walk; Woolwich Dockyard station is near Church Street and within walking distance; tube to North Greenwich (Jubilee Line) – the station is approximately two miles from the Thames Barrier; bus 161, 177, 180 or 472 via Greenwich – the stop is at the top of Eastmoor Street | Hours For Information Centre hours, opening times and guided tours visit thamesbarriertheview@environment-agency.gov.uk | Tip To appreciate how extraordinary the high tide was on 7 January, 1928, head for Crowley's Wharf, which is situated on the river walk at the end of Crane Street by Hoskins Street, where there's a commemorative plaque with a gauge line.

96 __ Theatre of Wine

Stage for wines that 'have something to say'!

Greenwich was the first London neighbourhood to get a Theatre of Wine, and although there are now two more north of the river, this was the original – and, we think, the best. Founded in 2002 by former actor, wine connoisseur, aesthete and *bon vivant* Daniel Illsley, Theatre of Wine showcases wines not easily available elsewhere. Paradoxically inspired by the sheer ubiquity of wine in England, it was a reaction to the bulk-bought, boring creations in supermarkets and off licences. It represented an attempt to source and sell wines direct from small producers outside the mainstream, and really open people's eyes to the possibilities of good wine.

Almost 20 years on, Theatre of Wine is a real success story, with branches in Tufnell Park and Leyton, a wholesale business supplying London restaurants, and a loyal following who wouldn't shop for wine anywhere else. It's also added posh spirits and interesting craft beers to the range, including local products such as 'The Kernel' ales and Bermondsey Gin. With its large central table, the shop feels more like a meeting spot for local wine buffs than a retail outlet, although after a few minutes of browsing we guarantee you won't be able to resist a purchase or two.

The offer is predominantly European, beautifully and very accessibly curated, with recommendations ranging from the underrated wines of Franche-Comté to the best Vermouth for making Negronis and Manhattans. The selection of sparkling wines is particularly impressive, with several English varieties and lots of Champagne from small producers you won't have heard of – which, after all, is exactly the point.

Daniel is a showman and an enthusiast, and has assembled a team of like-minded wine-lovers, including his son, Tom. With Theatre of Wine, Daniel aims to bring good wine to the masses at affordable prices – and to that we raise a glass!

Address 75 Trafalgar Road, London, SE10 9TS, +44 (0)20 8858 6363, www.theatreofwine.com | **Getting there** Bus 108, 177, 180, 199 or 286; train to Maze Hill | **Hours** Mon – Sat 10am – 9pm, Sun noon – 6pm | **Tip** Perhaps the best way to experience Theatre of Wine is to participate in one of their weekly wine-tasting events – a chance to get up close and personal to wines that, as Daniel puts it, 'have something to say'!

97 Titanic Memorial Garden
Peaceful memorial to a maritime tragedy

It's a rather diminutive memorial for a major event, but the restrained prettiness of the Titanic Memorial Garden is a refreshing surprise, given the scale and longevity of the disaster. Made up of an array of plants that are traditionally used for remembrance – roses, rosemary, purple sage and golden yew – it was opened in 1995, on the 83rd anniversary of the sinking of the *Titanic,* by one Edith Haisman – who, along with her mother, had survived the epic sinking when she was just 15 years old. There's a street in Southampton named after her, where she died in 1997.

Everyone knows the story. The RMS *Titanic* sank on 15 April, 1912, while on its maiden voyage, after striking an iceberg off the coast of Newfoundland. It was the pride of the White Star Line, larger and more luxurious than any ship then in existence. Having been launched to much fanfare on 11 April, it set off from Southampton and heading for New York, where it was expected to arrive on the morning of 17 April. Built in Belfast's Harland & Wolff shipyard, the vessel attracted a high-class, wealthy clientele, all of whom were eager to be among the first to sample the unprecedented facilities available on board. These included a pool, gym, library and multiple restaurants – all standard offerings on the cruise ships of today, but a rare glimpse into the future at the time. The ship took around two hours to sink, and of around 2,200 passengers and crew, around 1,500 people died, most of them from immersion into the icy waters of the North Atlantic.

Tucked away behind the museum, the garden's simplicity is at odds with the horror of the *Titanic* tragedy. But somehow its granite plinth, topped with a bronze plaque commemorating the ship and 'all those who were lost with her', feels like precisely the right sort of memorial – modest, easy to miss, but with a quiet, moving power.

Address National Maritime Museum, London, SE10 9JL | Getting there Train to Greenwich or Maze Hill; DLR to Cutty Sark; bus 129, 177, 180, 188, 199, 286 or 386 to Greenwich town centre | Hours Daily 10am–5pm | Tip After you've looked at the memorial, pop into the Maritime Museum and see some of the artefacts that have been rescued from the Deep, including a revolver used by one of the officers to quell passenger unrest as the ship sank, and a rusty pocket watch, which stopped at the exact time – 3.07am – that its unfortunate owner (27-year-old Robert Howard) entered the water.

98_ Tom Cribb's Grave

Lion memorial fit for a World Champion fighter

Tom Cribb was the very first World Champion in bare-knuckle fighting – a brutal, bloody sport closely related to ancient combats. The first recorded English contest took place in 1681, after which bare-knuckle fighting persisted for 200 years, until new regulations insisted gloves be worn. By 1804, when Bristolian Tom Cribb arrived in London, fights had become a national obsession. Spectators bet vast amounts, and prize monies amounted to fortunes.

Cribb was 23 when he fled Bristol following an incident in which he seriously injured another man. To escape punishment, he signed on as a sailor. He travelled as far as London, where he decided to end his nautical career, switching to the more lucrative London prize fighting scene. Bending the truth a little, the newspapers described the pugilist as an undefeated champion, but in truth he had been defeated once, at the start of his career. Cribb was awarded the British title in 1810, but it's his two victories against Tom Molineaux – a former slave – that won him posterity. Cribb was crowned World Champion having won a second fight in 1811 – a contest that took place in Leicestershire in front of more than 20,000 people. He retired a hero aged 31, and died aged 67, above his son's bakery on Woolwich High Street. This followed three decades of various failed ventures: first as a coal merchant – the family trade – then as publican of the Union Arms in Panton Street, which is now named after him.

His grave stands alone, on a mound, in St Mary's Garden, Woolwich, the location of a place of worship for 1,000 years. Cribb's memorial is a majestic lamenting lion with its head high, resting its paw on an engraved urn and a fighter's belt. Weather-beaten headstones line the walls of the public park, and the views of the ferries are lovely. It's a stunningly peaceful resting place for this once famous man who lived such a violent life.

Address St Mary Magdalene Church Park, Greenlaw Street, London, SE18 5AR |
Getting there St Mary's Park is behind the New Wine Church on the roundabout;
by train, the park is equally distanced from Woolwich Dockyard and Woolwich Arsenal;
bus 161, 177, 180 or 472 | Tip Central Woolwich, although sadly neglected, is well-
worth a visit for its Art Deco buildings, such as the Town Hall, with its magnificent
bonbon-box interior, and the UK's very first McDonald's, which opened in Powis Street
in 1974 – there's even a plaque on the shop front commemorating the event.

99 Trafalgar Tavern

Whitebait suppers and 'Our Mutual Friend'

Greenwich has always been a great place for pubs, and its riverside establishments stand out: none more so than the bow-fronted Regency dame that is the Trafalgar Tavern, which occupies one of Greenwich's most elegant riverside buildings, just a hop, skip and jump away from the Naval College. Still very much a pub, its terrace is usually thronged with happy drinkers on summer evenings, who gather around the statue of Nelson outside to gaze out over the river. Joining them is hard to resist, and in any case it's worth the price of a pint just to have a peek at its Grade II-listed interior.

The pub was purpose-built as a hostelry in 1837, to a grand design by Joseph Kay – clerk of works to Greenwich Hospital, and best-known as the designer of Greenwich town centre, where he re-mod-elled the market place. It was one of the top places to dine of its day, famous for a fish-filled glass tank from which gentlemen could choose their supper: turtles, eels, and in particular whitebait, were common items on the menu. Known to be a favourite with mem-bers of the Whig party (Tories apparently used to dine at the Cutty Sark), it became well-known for its annual whitebait suppers, which were attended by the most successful politicians of the day. It was also a regular haunt of Charles Dickens, who held a celebratory dinner here in 1842, after his return from America. Dickens liked it so much he made it the scene of a wedding reception in *Our Mutual Friend*.

The Trafalgar Tavern has been through some difficult times over the years. It closed down in 1915, was later used as a retirement home for mariners, and a seamen's hostel, until finally returning to some-thing like its original function in the 1960s, becoming a swanky bar and restaurant. With several changes of ownership over the years, it is now a regular pub again – albeit one with spacious ground floor rooms that enjoy magnificent views of the river.

Address Park Row, London, SE10 9NW, +44 (0)20 3887 9886, www.trafalgartavern.co.uk |
Getting there Bus 108, 177, 180, 199 or 286; train to Maze Hill; DLR to Cutty Sark, then a
short walk along the riverside path | Hours Mon–Fri noon–11pm, Sat 11am–midnight,
Sun 11am–10.30pm | Tip The upstairs Nelson Room is the Trafalgar's real treasure, used for
weddings and functions these days but worth a look if you get the chance. There are floor-to-
ceiling windows overlooking the river, and French balconies on which you can lounge with a
drink and imagine yourself back in the day, shooting the breeze after a delicious whitebait supper.

100__Trinity Hospital

South London's dinkiest almshouses

A diminutive, almost Ruritanian Gothic-style castle, the almshouses of Trinity Hospital are an odd contrast with the over-sized power station next door – a perfect manifestation of the paradoxical nature of this part of the river, where the ceremonial and historical sit cheek-by-jowl with the functional and industrial.

Trinity Hospital still fulfils its original purpose as a retirement home, and its courtyard, chapel and gardens look much as they did when the hospital was built in 1613 by Henry Howard, the Earl of Northampton, as almshouses to house around 20 pensioners. Entry requirements were strict: it was declared with great formality that occupants could not be 'a common beggar, drunkard, whore-hunter, nor unclean, blind or an idiot'. Now owned by the Mercers Company, they've presumably relaxed the policy slightly, and at the same time increased Trinity Hospital's size by adding a modern extension at the end of the garden, which is where the main entrance is these days – on Old Woolwich Road.

This part of the river has been particularly prone to flooding over the years, as evidenced by the plaques set into the wall outside the old building, which record the extraordinary high tides of 1874 and 1928, when the Thames burst its banks in multiple places, and the wall was largely destroyed, leaving Trinity Hospital deep in water. Following the completion of the Thames Barrier in 1982, this sort of thing is unlikely to happen again, but this part of the river is still vulnerable and flood-prevention works are ongoing.

Above all, this is a great place to take in the horseshoe of the Thames as it curves around the bottom of the Isle of Dogs. There are a couple of benches raised on plinths so you can sit and look out at the river, across to the swish apartments and high-rise offices of Dock-lands on the opposite bank, and the low dome of the O2 to the right.

Address Old Woolwich Road, London, SE10 9AS | **Getting there** Train to Maze Hill; DLR to Cutty Sark; bus 129, 177, 180, 188, 199, 286 or 386 to Greenwich town centre | **Hours** Annual open days only | **Tip** Take a look at the mysterious artwork on the wall outside the power station – a sort of ceramic cartoon telling the story of a little boy taking his dog for a walk by the river, where he finds a magic can of drink and meets a mystical creature. Commissioned by Greenwich Council for the Millennium, it's a lovely, rather whimsical piece of work by Amanda Hinge.

101 Up the Creek

Still one of London's best comedy venues

Dating back to the glory days of alternative comedy, having been founded in a derelict church hall in the early 1990s by local comedian Malcom Hardee, Up the Creek is still going strong after almost 30 years, albeit looking rather different since being merged into the new development along this stretch of Creek Road. It is, however, good to see its brick façade and windows emerge again after being covered with purple paint for over a decade.

Now deceased, Hardee was something of a legend in this part of south-east London, first of all running comedy sessions at the infamous Tunnel Club close to the entrance of the Blackwall Tunnel, then moving to Up the Creek in 1991. He was notorious for many things – including being investigated by the police for stealing Freddie Mercury's 40th birthday cake, and a unique impersonation of Charles de Gaulle, which involved balancing his spectacles on the top of his penis. At Up the Creek, Hardee picked the acts and acted as MC every weekend, before parting company in 2001. Living in a houseboat up the river in Rotherhithe, he sadly drowned in 2005 whilst trying to find his way home by boat after a particularly heavy drinking session at his floating pub – the Wibbly Wobbly; he was still clutching a bottle of beer when found. The club hosts a mural of the Last Supper in the upstairs bar, which features Hardee as Christ, surrounded by 1980s comedy and music circuit pals such as Dawn French, Jennifer Saunders, Ben Elton, Julian Clary and local mucker Jools Holland. With such a long and illustrious heritage, Up the Creek remains one of the capital's best places to see comedy. It hosts a packed bill every Friday and Saturday night, with open mic nights on Thursdays and Sundays presented by Malcom's stepson Will Briggs. As well as laughter, it also serves excellent burgers and its own home-brewed ales in its two bars.

Address 302 Creek Road, London, SE10 9SW, +44 (0)20 8858 4581, www.up-the-creek.com | **Getting there** DLR to Cutty Sark; train to Greenwich or bus to any central Greenwich stop, then a short walk | **Hours** Thu–Sun shows from 8pm (doors open at 7pm) | **Tip** Creek Road is named after Deptford Creek – basically another name for where the tributary of the river Ravensbourne enters the Thames. Just a short walk from Up the Creek, Deptford Bridge traverses the Ravensbourne at exactly the spot where the Romans forded the river in ancient times – the 'Deep Ford' which gave the district its name.

102 — The Valley

Spiritual home of 'The Addicks'

Home to south-east London's Charlton Athletic, The Valley enjoys a reputation arguably greater than that of its tenants. For many years it had one of the highest capacities in the league due to its huge east terrace, which was for years one of the world's largest. It even hosted the loudest ever rock concert in 1976, featuring The Who. And it became a political issue when the Valley Party stood in the 1990 local elections, aiming to persuade the local council to accept the team's return after a five-year exile. They won, the council agreed to the stadium's renovation, and The Valley is now a well-appointed all-seater venue with a capacity of just over 27,000.

Known as 'The Addicks', Charlton is a family-friendly club that's active in football's anti-racism campaigns, and known for producing gifted young players, most of whom soon move on to larger clubs. While Charlton's supporters wouldn't have it any other way, considering themselves unique among English fans, prising them away from their spiritual home, a proposal occasionally mooted by opportunistic owners, would be difficult indeed.

The first games were played at The Valley in 1919, and Charlton became one of England's biggest clubs under the legendary Jimmy Seed, finally winning the FA Cup in 1947. The club was less successful in the 1950s and 1960s, with constant speculation regarding The Valley – a precious slice of real estate. Eventually the club ran out of cash and was forced to leave in 1985, but returned in 1992, then enjoying Premier League glory under Alan Curbishley.

The club's history is documented in its museum, located in the North Stand – still affectionately known as the 'Covered End'. After visiting the museum, go to the main entrance of the West Stand, where you'll find a bronze statue of the club's veteran goalkeeper, Sam Bartram, who holds the record for Charlton appearances: a massive 579!

Address Floyd Road, London, SE7 8BL | **Getting there** Train to Charlton; bus 161, 177, 188 or 472 stop either outside Charlton or on the nearby Woolwich Road | **Hours** Museum open first Friday of the month 11am–3pm during the football season, 11am–1pm on Saturday match-days | **Tip** South-east London's other big club was of course Arsenal, founded by armaments workers from Woolwich Arsenal – first as 'Dial Square', then 'Royal Arsenal' – but they moved north of the river in 1913. Football fans can see some leftover terraces of the Invicta Stadium in some of the gardens of the houses on and around Mineral Street in Plumstead, or by visiting a patch of ground off Nathan Way, near Plumstead bus garage, which was the home of the Manor Ground – the club's first stadium.

103   Vanbrugh Castle

A quirky architect come spy designed this folly

When strolling in the less touristy part of Greenwich, known as East Greenwich, the name Sir John Vanbrugh is much in evidence. The Vanbrugh Tavern bears his name, as do many local businesses, and even a hill. But how did an architect and playwright from Chester come to be immortalised in Greenwich?

Born in 1664, the fourth-oldest child of 20, John made his own success. Yet throughout his life he benefited from strong business connections with the gentry, acquired early on through his father's sugar refining and trading business. In his youth, he was a strong supporter of the Whig Party and parliamentary democracy. He acted as a spy for William of Orange, was arrested in 1688, and spent four years in French prisons, including La Bastille. His time spent in France informed his choices when he later became an architect. Indeed, there is a little '*je ne sais quoi*' of the infamous Parisian French prison in the aspect of Vanbrugh Castle.

In his mid-fifties, Sir John married Henrietta Yarburgh, who was half his age. The couple spent most of their life in Greenwich, where he had been appointed Surveyor of the Royal Greenwich Hospital. Vanbrugh, who was responsible for two major buildings of the time – Blenheim Palace and Castle Howard – was now designing his family home. The Grade I-listed building, dated c.1718, is now private property, and can be admired from its gate on Maze Hill. When one of the castle wings recently came up for sale it was described as a miniature Scottish, tower house – although, with its baroque front, plum-coloured bricks, Doric porch, crenelated round towers and conical copper roof, it looks very much like a cross between a Gothic castle and a Medieval folly. To add to the mystery, a derelict tunnel is believed to run between the castle and the park. Originally to transport water, we can only speculate what else made its way through.

Address 121 Maze Hill, London, SE10 8XQ | Getting there Train to Maze Hill, from the station road turn left onto Maze Hill, then a five-minute walk up the hill | Tip Folly Pond is a small pond outside Greenwich Park on Blackheath, in its heyday it was a boating lake. It has now returned to nature and is an excellent spot for experimental photographers.

104_Veteran Trees
Greenwich's gentle giants

There are nearly 4,000 trees in the royal park, most old, some ancient. Visitors will have heard about Queen Elizabeth's Oak (see ch. 69), but there is more to the Veteran Trees than the famous 13th-century oak. Between 1661 and 1669, Charles II commissioned the planting of several avenues, which included sweet chestnuts and elms. The large sweet chestnut trees that border the road as you enter through Blackheath gate are a good example.

For this task, the King commissioned André Le Nôtre, Louis XIV's head gardener, famous for landscaping the Palace of Versailles' parterres. Le Nôtre designed a formal French-style layout, and over the years the avenues have been replanted as trees have died. Of the original planting, 62 trees remain, including sweet chestnuts, a few oaks, a sycamore, and a cedar. One of these giants can be admired in the flower garden by one of the gates.

Greenwich Royal Park plays an important ecological role. Its stock is unique, and it's home to complex communities of plants, fungi, insects and microorganisms. As the trees grow very old, their hearts decay. To the untrained eye they look battered, but there's still plenty of life in them. In the 1950s one of the sweet chestnut avenues was replanted with horse chestnuts. It's a fine balancing act for the park management to keep these old giants alive and attractive.

In the 1970s, diseased elms were replaced by more resistant species, but today the avenues are again under threat, as new diseases such as Bleeding Canker and Phytophthora attack the chestnuts. Thus, as part of a project due for completion in 2024, a total of 308 new trees are to be planted, with seeds collected from the veterans being grown in the nursery. The new trees will add to existing stock, and replace old ones. With all this care, the chestnuts could live as long as the Hundred-Horse Chestnut of Sicily, estimated to be 3,000 years old.

Address Chestnut Avenue, Greenwich Park, London, SE10 8QY, www.royalparks.org.uk/parks/greenwich-park | **Getting there** From the Greenwich Park entrance, take the first large avenue; as a guide, the statue of General Wolfe is at the top; train to Greenwich; bus 53, 54, 129, 177, 180, 188, 199, 286 or 386; by boat to Greenwich Pier; DLR to Cutty Sark, then walk through the market to St Mary's Gate, King William Walk, or Circus Gate on Crooms Hill | **Hours** See website for current information on visiting | **Tip** The original Le Notre planting included a set of giant steps – these remain partly visible today, and will be restored along with the new planting project. At the top, don't miss the viewing area of One Tree Hill, which provides one of the best views of London.

105 Well Hall Pleasaunce

Superb garden with Tudor and literary connections

As you walk through the Italian Gate of the Well Hall Pleasaunce in Eltham, it doesn't take much imagination to be transported to a beautiful Tuscan garden. This award-winning space has historical connections to the Tudors, gardens with a variety of themes, a bowling green and play area, water features, ancient bee-boles and even a literary and a railway association.

The site was already occupied back in the mid-1200s, but from the early 1500s to 1733, it belonged to the House of Roper – first to William, Henry VIII's Attorney General, and his wife, Margaret. Margaret Roper was a respected writer, and the daughter of Sir Thomas More. When the estate was sold, the residence was torn down and replaced with a property, rather confusingly, also called Well Hall. This was home to Edith Nesbit, author of *The Railway Children*. A plaque marks the site where it once stood. Nesbit recreated the house in one of her works, with its panelled room, great hall and vaulted cellar. Many of the Nesbits' literary friends visited to party in these grounds, including H. G. Wells and Bernard Shaw.

It was from 1930 onwards, when the land was sold to Woolwich Borough Council, that the planting in the garden really flourished. The aim was to create a public park for the growing number of Eltham residents to enjoy. Large Mount Atlas cedar, London plane, dark yews, sycamore and ginkgo are just a few of the species among the majestic ornamental trees. Look out for the restored rockery and the wildflower meadow, the rose garden, and the parterre designed in the shape of a Tudor Rose. Ponds, fountains, a moat, and surreal animal sculptures all add to the interest. Although a beautiful landscape in all seasons, in late spring to early summer the wisteria arch comes into its own – a spectacular horticultural feature with cascades of purple flowers. Grand surroundings for a walk.

Address 59 Well Hall Road, London, SE9 6SZ, +44 (0)20 8856 0100, www.wellhall.org.uk |
Getting there Train to Eltham; bus 132, 161 or 286 | **Hours** Closes Nov–Jan 4pm,
Mar–Apr 6pm, May 8pm, Jun–Aug 9pm, Sep 7pm, Oct 6pm | **Tip** Feeling peckish or want
to treat the family, the Tudor Barn in the park cater for park users, the building dates back to
the 16th century and the service is a delight.

106 West Greenwich Library

'Let there be light'

Libraries are central to the borough's cultural life. With 12 branches, the provision is comprehensive, and there is always something on offer, from children's story times to author events, via the annual Summer Reading Challenge. As a tourist, though, the best place to head for is West Greenwich Library, with its beautiful interior.

This edifice is a 'must-see' place of architectural heritage. Situated in the heart of town, the attractive red-brick building has a baroque appearance, with its unusual open cupola flanked by eight Tuscan columns. A cartouche on the front explains that it was *The Gift of Andrew Carnegie Esq.*. Carnegie was richer than J. D. Rockefeller, and was for several years the richest American. The philanthropist considered enlightenment as a genuine remedy to the ills affecting the human race, and as such, gifted a fortune to public library buildings. His motto was 'Let there be light', which also describes the library's wow-factor. As you enter it all looks perfectly normal: large rooms with standard library furniture, bookshelves and computers. Yet the whole place is bathed in natural light, and when you look up you discover the source of the illumination: high above is a round balcony, with three beautiful domes that transform the place into something spectacular. Each dome is made of a hexagonal cupola comprised of around 20 windows. Two are blue, the other terracotta, enhanced by flower and fruit crown mouldings.

Once outside, stroll next door to the clock tower. The building was Greenwich Town Hall before council services moved to Woolwich. The glass near the top of the tower was intended as an observation deck with river views. Nobody has been allowed inside for a long time, but the mosaic ceiling in the side entrance remains visible, combining maritime themes and zodiac symbols. It's another opportunity to look up and smile.

Address 146 Greenwich High Road, London, SE10 8NN, +44 (0)20 8858 4289 | Getting there Train to Greenwich, then a five-minute walk; bus 177, 188 or 199; DLR to Cutty Sark; boat to Greenwich Pier | Hours Check website for details: www.better.org.uk/library/london/greenwich/west-greenwich-library | Tip Opposite the Town Hall there's another hidden gem: a long ceramics mural situated between the Post Office and HSBC buildings. Be aware, though, that the alley entrance is easy to miss. It connects Straightsmouth and Greenwich High Road.

107 William IV Statue
The 'Sailor King' gives an unexpected eyeful

The imposing statue of King William IV just outside the National Maritime Museum is a good meeting point for those heading into central Greenwich. The third son of George III, he succeeded his elder brother, George IV, in 1830, and reigned for seven years – a time which saw the Great Reform Act passed, and the abolition of slavery.

Known as the 'Sailor King', due to his distinguished naval career, it's appropriate that William occupies a significant spot in Greenwich. It's claimed he was offered no special privileges despite being third in line for the throne, but served as an able seaman and late midshipman in Gibraltar and the Caribbean, and became a close friend of Nelson – so close that he gave away Nelson's bride on the great hero's wedding day. William rose to become Admiral of the Fleet, and eventually Lord High Admiral of England. He also achieved some notoriety for a long affair with one Dorothea Bland – a famous actress known as Mrs Jordan, with whom he had no fewer than 10 illegitimate children. They are said to have been extremely happy together, but as a possible future king he was forced to break with her in 1814. He agreed to pay a stipend on condition she didn't return to the stage, but this she did, and thus died in poverty in France two years later. William later married the German princess Adelaide. The couple had just two children, both of whom died in infancy, which meant his beloved niece Victoria ascended to the throne on his death in 1837. Adelaide's name lives on in the South Australian city founded by William shortly before his death.

The statue itself originally stood near London Bridge on King William Street, but was moved to its current location in the 1930s – a much quieter and more dignified spot. It remains the artwork people love to snigger at, however, when viewed from a certain angle, William looks unusually well endowed!

Address King William Walk, London, SE10 9JL | Getting there Train to Greenwich or Maze Hill; DLR to Cutty Sark; bus 129, 177, 180, 188, 199, 286 or 386 to Greenwich town centre | Hours You can see the statue at any time, but to get up close you'll have to visit when the Maritime Museum is open, daily 10am–5pm | Tip There's a portrait of William IV in full dress uniform in the Queen's House, painted in 1837, shortly before he died.

108_ Woodlands Farm

A fun day out

To have free and easy access to almost 90 acres of farmland, just a few miles away from city life, is as surprising as it is remarkable. Woodlands Farm, created in 1800 from a dense forest called Bushy Lees Wood, is the largest working city farm in the UK. Thanks to two centuries of adaptation, it has survived attempts at development, and even a plan for the East London river crossing.

Nowadays, the Woodlands Farm Trust, known to locals as Shooter's Hill Farm, is a charity run mainly by volunteers. It gives visitors the chance to see the inner workings of a farmyard, and an opportunity to get up close to native fauna and flora. Lambs and pigs are firm favourites, and cows answer to bucolic names such as Clover or Snowdrop. Plumpy Buff Orpington chickens strut with a stately air, and four-horned sheep from the Isle of Man constantly amaze visitors.

There's a regular programme of events throughout the year, such as spring bird walks, shelter building and pond dipping. There are also orienteering courses for those who are directionally-challenged, or too reliant on their GPS. The farm not only educates, but also offers a unique opportunity to conserve the landscape and promote biodiversity. A 600-year old hedge provides one of London's most diverse wildlife habitats. It's home to foxes, skylarks and kestrels, and produces a variety of bays and berries, which are turned into delicious chutneys and unusual jams.

There's also a farm shop, and six times a year the volunteers fling open the doors to welcome in the wider community. Farm-goers look forward to Lambing Day in the spring, which offers a chance to meet new-born balls of fluff, and Apple Day in October, when they can taste many varieties of the fruit, and work a press to make delicious juice. Father Christmas is a regular visitor in December, with Bob the Pony given the honour of pulling his sleigh.

Address 331 Shooter's Hill, London, DA16 3RP, +44 (0)20 8319 8900, thewoodlandsfarmtrust.org | Getting there Train to Welling, Blackheath, Lewisham, then bus 89 or 486, with the nearest stop Farm Gate | Tip There's a farmers' market every Sunday morning near Blackheath railway station.

109__Woolwich Ferry

Free commute with a sea-breeze in your hair

There has been a ferry crossing at this point for hundreds of years. Its origins can be traced back to 1308, when a waterman under the name of William de Wicton ran it. Since then, its history has been as tumultuous as the Thames tidal currents. In 1884, after a lot of public pressure, the charges for crossing by ferry were dropped. Five years later, Woolwich threw a large party with procession and banners when the link reopened. That weekend the rail company carried 25,000 people to its North Woolwich terminus, most of whom were intent on riding the only boat on that day, *The Gordon*. Then the ships were paddle steamers and suitable for horse-drawn traffic, but with the introduction of the car, operations became difficult. The vessels were unable to cope with the increase in weight.

In 1963, the fleet was eventually replaced by diesel river-buses, and 2018 saw an upgrade with the arrival of two hybrid electric vessels. This time there was no ribbon cutting, and it soon became evident that the curse had stuck. Every day was a crossing lottery, leaving commuters wondering whether the *Ben Woollacott* or *Dame Vera Lynn* would actually make it. Of course, if a journey is cancelled, foot passengers can always use the Woolwich tunnel – the lesser-known foot tunnel under the Thames, built at the same time and looking very similar to its famous counterpart in Greenwich.

By early 2020, history repeated itself as, like in 1844, inadequate management amplified the disruptions. These became so serious that Transport for London sacked the contractors and started running operations in-house. One day in April of that year, at dusk, one of the ships demonstrated strange behaviour, starting to twirl, all lights blazing, making doughnut shapes at mid-crossing. Twitter went wild! It transpired that the ferry-men were thanking the NHS staff for their work during the pandemic.

Address New Ferry Approach, London, SE19 6DX, +44 (0)20 8853 9400 | **Getting there** Train to Woolwich Dockyard; bus 177 or 180 to Marlton Street | **Hours** Mon–Sat 7am–7pm, Sun 11.30am–7.30pm; boat runs approximately every 25 minutes, subject to tide and weather | **Tip** The Mersey Ferry *Royal Iris*, made famous by Gerry and the Pacemakers with 'Ferry Cross the Mersey', is now partially sunk, and turning into a rusting wreck in her berth near the Thames Barrier.

110 Wuthering Heights
'It's me, Cathy, I've come home!'

You don't have to go to the atmospheric moors of Yorkshire to visit the house that inspired *Wuthering Heights*. Instead, visit Eltham, where there's a splendid residence bearing the name of Emily Brontë's best-known novel. The attractive six-bedroom home belonged to the singer Kate Bush for around 20 years, before being placed on the market in 2014 for nearly £3 million. At the time, the estate agent's description didn't specify whether Kathy's ghost would be haunting the property, as she does in the song.

The singer's former dwelling is a solitary spot surrounded by extensive grounds, and obscured by trees and walls. Nevertheless, the public can appreciate its wrought iron gate emblazoned with the name *'Wuthering Heights'*, and glimpse the large, red-brick property. During her time living in Eltham, the enigmatic singer was something of a recluse, but treated like one of the locals: her home was referred to simply as 'Kate Bush's house'. Bush was born in Bexleyheath, and shares the same birth date as Emily Brontë. She grew up in a farmhouse in East Wickham, and was the first female singer to achieve a UK number one with a self-penned song. In 1978, when she released the single that would propel her to fame, she was already well known locally: the young lady in a long red bohemian-style dress with ragged hemline had been performing in pubs for a while. She and the 'KT Bush Band' held their first rehearsal in the Arches Swimming Baths in Greenwich (as did another local band, Squeeze). Locals still remember her debut, which took place in March 1977 in front of around 30 people, in what was then The Rose of Lee – now the Dirty South.

The KT Bush Band is still playing tribute gigs in local community venues. Incidentally, Boy George, another 1980s singer with an outré dress-sense and a few number ones to his name, was also born locally; unlike Kate, however, he escaped suburbia as soon as possible.

Address Wuthering Heights, Court Road, London, SE9 5AG | Getting there The house, which is on private grounds, backs onto the golf club, and can be reached on foot in 15 minutes from Eltham High Street; train to Mottingham; tube to North Greenwich (Jubilee Line); bus 161 to Court Road | Tip Bob Hope is a son of Eltham too! There's a plaque in Craigton Road to commemorate the famous actor, who also rescued Eltham Little Theatre from closure when the church landlords raised the rent. In 1982, the theatre was renamed The Bob Hope Theatre.

111 Yuri Gagarin Statue

The man who circled the Earth came to rest here

The man who orbited the Earth in 108 minutes is celebrated on the grounds of the Royal Observatory next to the Planetarium. This is certainly a fitting place for a commemorative statue of the most famous cosmonaut, and the first human space explorer. The seven-metre-high monument shows a young Gagarin looking proud and purposeful in his spacesuit, standing astride the globe. Made of zinc and surrounded by the tall windows of the observatory, the statue gives an overall impression of a man in a space capsule. The monument marks the 50th anniversary of Gagarin's voyage into space aboard Vostok 1 on 12 April, 1961. The statue is an exhibition copy of a Russian sculpture made in 1984 by Anatoly Novikov, one of the chief sculptors of the Stalingrad Memorial. His original Gagarin piece is on show in the town of Lyubertsy, just outside Moscow, where Gagarin trained as a steel foundry worker.

This elegant sculpture was a gift to Britain from the Russian space agency Roscosmos, to mark another golden anniversary: 50 years since the cosmonaut visited London, on 14 July, 1961. Gagarin visited London as part of a world tour, with the newspapers of the time reporting that the cosmonaut had been astonished by the public's reception.

Initially, the statue was installed on the Mall, in central London, where thousands gathered to catch a glimpse of the space-faring visitor. At only 27, Gagarin had captured the imagination of millions across the world with his exploit. His London visit was so successful that it was extended twice. Novikov's statue stayed for 12 months near Admiralty Arch, where it stood facing the statue of Captain Cook. Then, in 2013, it was moved to Greenwich on the world's prime meridian, where by strange coincidence the Gagarin statue was reunited with that of Captain Cook, making this the place to visit to pay your respects to two legendary explorers.

Address Royal Observatory, Astronomy Café, Gagarin Terrace, London, SE10 8XJ |
Getting there Car parking available for visitors with disabilities only – limited pre-booked
spaces are available mailto:bookings@rmg.co.uk; the Royal Observatory is at the top of
a fairly steep hill; allow 15 minutes on foot from King William Walk; DLR or boat to
Cutty Sark; train to Maze Hill or Blackheath, then a 20-minute flat walk across the heath |
Tip Eltham cemetery features some interesting memorials, including the figure of a man
dressed in flying gear. The gravestone on which the sculpture stands is that of E. F. Bennett,
an airman who lost his life when flying solo in 1938 (Woods Way, London, SE9 2RF).

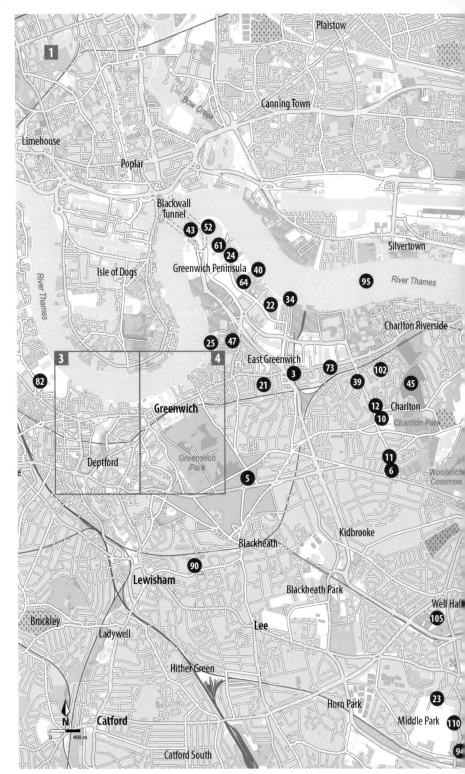

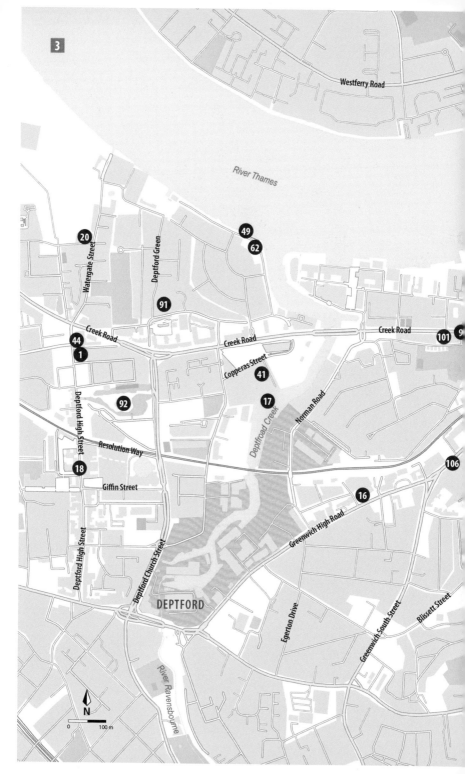

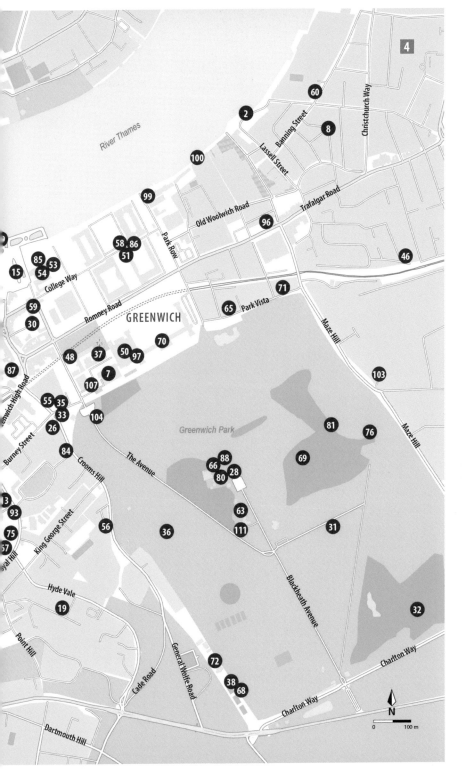

Solange Berchemin
111 Places in the Lake District
That You Shouldn't Miss
ISBN 978-3-7408-0378-0

John Sykes, Birgit Weber
111 Places in London
That You Shouldn't Miss
ISBN 978-3-95451-346-8

Nicola Perry, Daniel Reiter
33 Walks in London
That You Shouldn't Miss
ISBN 978-3-95451-886-9

Kirstin von Glasow
111 Gardens in London
That You Shouldn't Miss
ISBN 978-3-7408-0143-4

Laura Richards, Jamie Newson
111 London Pubs and Bars
That You Shouldn't Miss
ISBN 978-3-7408-0893-8

Emma Rose Barber, Benedict Flett
111 Churches in London
That You Shouldn't Miss
ISBN 978-3-7408-0901-0

Ed Glinert, Marc Zakian
111 Places in London's East End
That You Shouldn't Miss
ISBN 978-3-7408-0752-8

Rob Ganley, Ian Williams
111 Places in Coventry
That You Shouldn't Miss
ISBN 978-3-7408-1044-3

Martin Booth,
Barbara Evripidou
111 Places in Bristol
That You Shouldn't Miss
ISBN 978-3-7408-0898-3

Kim Revill, Alesh Compton
**111 Places in Leeds
That You Shouldn't Miss**
ISBN 978-3-7408-0754-2

Julian Treuherz,
Peter de Figueiredo
**111 Places in Manchester
That You Shouldn't Miss**
ISBN 978-3-7408-0753-5

Julian Treuherz,
Peter de Figueiredo
**111 Places in Liverpool
That You Shouldn't Miss**
ISBN 978-3-95451-769-5

Michael Glover,
Richard Anderson
**111 Places in Sheffield
That You Shouldn't Miss**
ISBN 978-3-7408-0022-2

Katherine Bebo, Oliver Smith
**111 Places in Poole
That You Shouldn't Miss**
ISBN 978-3-7408-0598-2

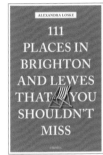

Alexandra Loske
**111 Places in Brighton and
Lewes That You Shouldn't Miss**
ISBN 978-3-7408-0255-4

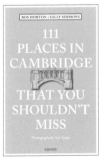

Rosalind Horton,
Sally Simmons, Guy Snape
**111 Places in Cambridge
That You Shouldn't Miss**
ISBN 978-3-7408-0147-2

Justin Postlethwaite
**111 Places in Bath
That You Shouldn't Miss**
ISBN 978-3-7408-0146-5

Gillian Tait
**111 Places in Edinburgh
That You Shouldn't Miss**
ISBN 978-3-95451-883-8

Tom Shields, Gillian Tait
111 Places in Glasgow
That You Shouldn't Miss
ISBN 978-3-7408-0256-1

Gillian Tait
111 Places in Fife
That You Shouldn't Miss
ISBN 978-3-7408-0597-5

Laszlo Trankovits
111 Places in Jerusalem
That You Shouldn't Miss
ISBN 978-3-7408-0320-9

Andrea Livnat,
Angelika Baumgartner
111 Places in Tel Aviv
That You Shouldn't Miss
ISBN 978-3-7408-0263-9

Alexia Amvrazi,
Diana Farr Louis, Diane Shugart,
Yannis Varouhakis
111 Places in Athens
That You Shouldn't Miss
ISBN 978-3-7408-0377-3

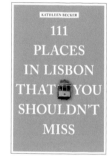

Kathleen Becker
111 Places in Lisbon
That You Shouldn't Miss
ISBN 978-3-7408-0383-4

Catrin George Ponciano
111 Places along the Algarve
That You Shouldn't Miss
ISBN 978-3-7408-0381-0

Thomas Fuchs
111 Places in Amsterdam
That You Shouldn't Miss
ISBN 978-3-7408-0023-9

Sybil Canac, Renée Grimaud,
Katia Thomas
111 Places in Paris
That You Shouldn't Miss
ISBN 978-3-7408-0159-5

Huge thanks to Martin who agreed in a nanosecond to co-write this book. I'm indebted to the explorers who launched their voyages from Greenwich, without them, Andy and I would have never come to live here, thank you. A very special thank you to baby Ophelia for her chirpy video-calls, can't wait to enjoy Greenwich nature reserves and other places off the beaten paths with her.
Solange Berchemin

Big thanks to my co-conspirator Solange for being a fabulous co-author and for getting me involved in the first place. Also to Caroline for reading, good ideas and accompanying me on trips to Greenwich's lesser-known corners, and to Sonny, Daisy and Lucy for walks in the park and by the river. Most of all, though, to my mum, who brought me back to Greenwich, and never liked to leave.
Martin Dunford

I'd like to thanks Solange and Martin for including me on their journey through places I never knew existed!
Karin Tearle

And...
Our warmest thanks to Karin Tearle for her success in taking great photos in the teeth of winter and a global pandemic; to all the business-owners and every single person who gifted us their time and their stories, answered our queries and generally smoothed the way; to Alistair Layzell for kicking off the process; to Martin Sketchley for his swift edits; and to Laura Olk at Emons Publishers for being brilliant at what she does and supporting us throughout.

Solange Berchemin was born in Lyon, France. Her Library Science degree at university marked the start of her adventures with words and stories. She moved to Greenwich with her partner three decades ago. She works as a food and travel journalist for major national publications and an international TV channel. But, nothing compares to her time as a columnist at *The Greenwich Visitor*. She is the author of seven books among which is *111 Places in the Lake District That You Shouldn't Miss*. To read her complete biography go to www.solangeberchemin.com.

Martin Dunford lives in Greenwich and is one of the founders of the international travel guide series *Rough Guides*. He is the author of more than 10 guidebooks and was the publisher of *Rough Guides* for many years, before going on to found the UK travel and accommodation website www.coolplaces.co.uk. Martin also works as a freelance travel writer, writing regularly about the UK, Belgium, Holland and Italy, among other destinations, and is a trustee of the Norfolk charity, The Broads Trust. He also co-owns the popular Greenwich restaurant, Buenos Aires Café.

Karin Tearle has a BA in French and Italian from Goldsmiths University of London. She lived and worked in Bordeaux, France for several years before returning to the UK and has lived in Greenwich for 15 years. Karin is a trustee of the Rwanda Development Trust and also manages a listed building in historic Greenwich. She is a passionate amateur photographer and is membership and social secretary of Aperture Woolwich Photographic Society, one of the oldest clubs in the country.